Seeing through Our Tears

Seeing through Our Tears

WHY WE CRY, HOW WE HEAL

DANIEL G. BAGBY

Augsburg
MINNEAPOLIS

SEEING THROUGH OUR TEARS
Why We Cry, How We Heal

Cover design by David Meyer
Book design by Michelle L. Norstad

Library of Congress Cataloging-in-Publication Data
Bagby, Daniel G.
  Seeing through our tears : why we cry, how we heal / by Daniel G. Bagby.
    p. cm.
  Includes bibliographical references.
  ISBN 0-8066-3731-5 (alk. paper)
  1. Crying—Religious aspects—Christianity. I. Title.
BV4909.B34 1999
248.8'6—dc21   98-50114
                                                                      CIP

Manufactured in the U.S.A.   AF 9-3731

03   02   01   00   99   1   2   3   4   5   6   7   8   9   10

TABLE OF CONTENTS

INTRODUCTION

TEARS ARE ONE OF THE MOST EXPRESSIVE WAYS in which we communicate. We cry for many different reasons. From the moment we were born, our limited vocabulary required tears to express hunger, discomfort, or fatigue. From infancy through adulthood, tears are companions during some of the most difficult moments in our life. They often reveal what we cannot put into words.

Tears were designed for every age in life. Though we have often misunderstood them to belong only to children, they have always been the language of the soul at every stage of living. Tears have celebrated our joys, stated our frustrations, and carried our grief. Tears have presided over the most significant moments in the human journey.

And yet, for all their familiarity, our tears have also mystified and bewildered us. Shrouded in mystery and surprise, our tears have told us many tales and spoken many languages. Tears are never meaningless. Acquainted with our deepest longings and highest aspirations, tears have conveyed anger, ecstasy, fatigue, fear, loneliness, pain, relief, and joy. Tears clothe our hearts and souls with words; they share the language of our inner selves.

Tears must therefore be understood. The rich variety of our tears requires interpretation. Our tears unveil the diversity of our emotions and the complexity of issues and values that impel us. To understand ourselves, we must understand our tears.

That is why I have written this book. For years I have watched people cry and learned from the vocabulary of their tears. As a chaplain, counselor, minister, and teacher, I have come to value what tears tell us. In the following pages, I hope you will also come to understand and appreciate the gift of tears.

It is not possible to describe all the meanings that our tears carry. The chapter divisions do not mean that our tears all have clearly defined purposes. Tears of anger, for example, may also contain frustration and fatigue. Tears of pain often carry sorrow. The following topical headings provide insight into some of the colorful and critical meanings of our tears:

Chapter 1: Tears of Anger. We need to understand the role of anger in our tears and to discover responsible ways to express the rage that sometimes stirs within us. We also need to understand how anger can be a form of care.

Chapter 2: Tears of Confession. What function does self-confrontation and confession have in the development of tears. How do we process remorse and regret in redemptive ways? How do we atone?

Chapter 3: Tears of Failure. How do we manage the reality of failure in life? How can we learn to find grace and hope to meet our imperfections?

Chapter 4: Tears of Fatigue. What part does exhaustion play in the issue of our tears? How can we become better stewards of our energy and opportunity?

Chapter 5: Tears of Fear. To what extent are we driven or controlled by anxieties and fears? How can we turn our vulnerability into strength?

Chapter 6: Tears of Frustration. To what degree do we manage the adversities of life so that they do not discourage or destroy us? How do we handle control and powerlessness in creative ways?

Chapter 7: Tears of Gratitude. Do we understand the tears that celebrate the unexpected good that surprises us in the midst of our sudden tragedies? Grace often brings tears of gladness during times of disaster.

Chapter 8: Tears of Loneliness. Isolation and alienation in relationships is a source of distress and disruption; how do we overcome our separation and emptiness?

Chapter 9: Tears of Manipulation. In what way do we try to evoke sympathy and pity, and how can we avoid using other people's feelings to gain affirmation and care? How do we learn to ask appropriately for what we need?

Chapter 10: Tears of Pain. How do we travel daily through chronic pain—and maintain hope? In what way is suffering instructive?

Chapter 11: Tears of Sorrow. We shed so many different tears for losses; how can we interpret the agony of tears born from sadness? How do we get past grief?

Chapter 12: When There Are No Tears. What does it mean when there are no tears? How do we wait creatively for tears—and our next dream?

The following pages are an introduction to the meaning of our tears. My hope is that each chapter may become a useful window through which we may see the world inside of us more clearly. I also hope that we will learn to value and affirm what we discover inside of us—for each of us, as I understand us, is made in the image of God.

Chapter 1

―――――――● ● ●―――――――

Tears of Anger

My tears burn on my cheeks;
my rage stirs deep inside—
next to the emptiness I feel
tis anger that won't hide!
And will it ever ebb?

SHE HAD CALLED TO MAKE AN APPOINTMENT. Because
of the distress and urgency in her voice, I shuffled my schedule to meet her that same day. I alerted our secretary that
Kathryn might need some privacy when she walked in, because
our church-office foyer was frequently an end-of-the-day congre-
gating place for college students.

Kathryn walked into my office with her head down and her
hands slightly hiding her face. She sank immediately into a chair
and began sobbing. As she cried, I looked carefully for signs of
embarrassment, despair, or preoccupation. After a moment, I
noticed the dark features around her eyes. She appeared to have
been in an accident—or beaten.

I had not known Kathryn long, but she had attended our
church since she came to law school in our city over two years
ago. She often slipped into the back of the sanctuary during the
worship hour, and always stopped to greet me at the back door
after the service. We had met two or three times during the
course of the year about vocational and personal issues; today
she had a lot more on her mind.

"I can't believe this, Dr. Bagby. . . . He knocked on my door, and I knew he was drunk. He just pushed his way into my apartment and . . . forced me down. I yelled at him—and he slapped me so hard I couldn't talk. . . . He told me I'd better shut up or he'd hurt me worse. . . . I struggled and fought"—here she showed me bruises on her arms and neck—"but he just over-powered me and forced me into the bedroom and raped me!"

Sobbing as she continued, Kathryn described her relation-ship to a fellow law student she had befriended months ago and had eventually become sexually involved with. Then he dropped her—only to reappear at her door a few weeks ago.

Kathryn wiped away her tears and continued to describe a physically and emotionally abusive relationship that had been going on for months. What had begun as an accidental and gen-tle liaison had turned into an oppressive sexual relationship. Kathryn struggled with fear and anger every time she saw the man now, but her last encounter had produced a rage that was almost impossible to cope with: she was so angry she could nei-ther study nor sleep well.

I asked Kathryn some important initial questions about her immediate medical condition and her sense of safety. She assured me she had no physical wounds that would not heal nat-urally—though a swollen jaw had her worried at first that a facial bone might be broken. I insisted she see a physician for a thor-ough medical examination, but this visibly disturbed her.

She was quite frightened about the possibility that anyone else would learn of the assault. As we talked further, she identi-fied two things: She feared that she might be "pushed" to identi-fy her attacker, and that he would do even more harm. She also told me her father could be physically aggressive and that if he knew this had happened to his daughter, he might want to hurt her attacker.

We talked for a few moments about medical options at school, in town, and back home, and about the confidentiality of each. I offered her the name of two doctors in the community who would see her and maintain the confidentiality she needed—even though they would ask her some direct questions for her own well-being. She assured me that she would see a doctor. I told her that I was going to follow up on this promise by calling the one she had chosen—both to confirm confidentiality and to ensure that she would take care of herself.

Next we talked about her personal sense of safety, beginning with where she was living. Her apartment was typical of those that university towns had available for graduate students, who often preferred to live by themselves. Kathryn had no roommate, but several law students lived in the complex. We rehearsed improved ways of reaching them, as well as campus security and the local police. Thanks to speed dialing, she could program her phone to dial several people for assistance. She also could lock her front door with a dead bolt and be more cautious when she entered and exited the building.

We discussed other details about her safety, as her tears were frequently interrupted by comments about anger and fear. We talked about her leaving town for a few days as soon as the marks were less noticeable—just to get some emotional "space." And then I turned to talk about her rage—the seething anger deep inside of her, behind the veil of tears.

Somewhere along the way, I said, some of us learned to shed tears when we were very angry. Sometimes there are no words for the rage inside us that screams for recognition when we've been wronged. Our tears of anger are the language we use as we struggle to give voice to the deep pain within us, the deep frustration of feeling abused.

Sometimes we feel robbed; sometimes we feel violated; sometimes we feel desecrated in our innermost self—the sacred, private places we hold dear. Often we flinch over the frustration that something very unfair has happened and that we feel helpless to overcome it. Whatever the feeling, the simmering turmoil inside of us is a keen warning that we are incensed and want to do something to relieve the pain.

*   *   *   *   *

In the televised evening news I watched a Bosnian refugee pounding her fists on a soldier's chest as she cried out over the agony of her family's death. Her husband and two of her children had just been the latest casualties in that fierce, divisive battle. She stretched out her angry hands and grabbed the first available human being who represented all those who had robbed her of what she most loved. Her tearful face expressed rage and astonishment: who were these people who had assumed the right to snatch away her joy?

What do we do with tears of anger? How do we help those who cry out because they are furious at injustice? How do we manage the bitter tears of rage? Several responses prove to be helpful, even redemptive. Here are some steps in working through the anger in our tears.

Acknowledging the Anger

People who are angry need to have their feelings recognized and validated. One of our common mistakes in taking responsible care of our anger is to try to ignore or argue with our own feelings. Feelings are legitimate emotions and they need to be recognized and identified as important. Ignored or neglected, anger only intensifies feelings of alienation and aggravates our pain.

Most of us have limited skills for managing and coping with the intense emotion of anger. In some cases, our own families have unintentionally taught us harmful ways to deal with it. We are taught to: avoid anger, ignore it, suppress it, deny it, or displace it. All such maneuvers disguise anger and conceal its destructive work. As a result of such camouflaging, pent up and neglected feelings can suddenly explode in the family circle and cause more damage because they are not understood and have gone untended.

The church, designed to be an institution of healing, has not provided much help in the stewardship of anger. Church-going families are often taught to pretend that anger does not exist or that it should be ignored. In addition, many congregations practice poor models of conflict and anger-resolution and, as a result, suffer from inadequate and harmful "family" habits when it comes to managing anger.

How can we handle anger in a healing way? The tears of anger some people shed are the result of caring deeply. Tears are an important physical evidence that we feel passionately about certain things. They are often the first clue that we are frustrated and disturbed, warnings that we need to take anger seriously and direct our feelings in responsible ways.

That is why those who cry in anger first need the affirmation that their deep feelings are important and should be identified: they need to know someone else knows how much they care, that their anger is real, and that it can be recognized and expressed without hurting anyone. People who shed tears of anger are enraged by certain events, and they don't want to be talked out of their feelings; they want someone to acknowledge them.

Not every angry person knows they are angry. Early family training and socialization have taught us to "swallow," hide, or mask some of our feelings. Anger is an emotion often labeled unacceptable or suppressed as undesirable. Like Archie Bunker's wife in the old *All in the Family* television series, most children have been told to "stifle" their anger and are then left to discover on their own what to do with their seething feelings.

Some people have been given permission to cry when they are angry but no permission to express anger. That is why some people cry when they are very angry. That is also why some people are surprised when we identify the feelings behind their tears as anger. Taught for so long to hide our anger, we have trouble recognizing our real feelings.

In addition, some deeply religious people struggle with their church's teachings about anger. Some faith communities have taught parishioners that anger in and of itself is sinful or bad; believers then struggle to disguise their anger and lose touch with important feelings over a period of time. Shame and guilt about anger then create more confusion for the angry Christian. What can we do about this bind?

Accepting the Passion of Anger

When we acknowledge anger for what it is, we are simply doing what believers in the Bible did from Genesis to Revelation. The Bible is very clear that God was often angry (Genesis 44:18, Exodus 4:14, Numbers 11:10, etc.), and that most of God's servants and prophets were angry at one time or other (Genesis 30:2, Exodus 32:19, I Samuel 20:34, etc.). Christ is visibly angry on several occasions in his ministry (Matthew 12:34, Mark 3:5, Luke 11:42ff, John 2:14-15, etc.), as are his followers (Acts 15:2, 15:38-9, I Corinthians 1:11, II Corinthians 2:4, etc.). Anger is a passionate emotion created by God, intended for responsible action. Anger can be an expression of care, such as God's anger with Israel, whom God loved, and Christ's anger at Peter, whom he loved enough to confront. Biblically, anger is also the natural response to abuse, manipulation, or neglect.

God was angry with Israel each time she abused the sacred relationship she had with the Lord and ignored the powerful gift of being chosen by God for important purposes (Numbers 32:13, Judges 2:14, 2:20, 3:8, II Kings 23:20, etc.). Christ was repeatedly angry with pharisees and others who abused and manipulated people with their power. He was infuriated with those who neglected the weak and oppressed the vulnerable, and said so (Matthew 23, Luke 6, and Luke 11 each carries a series of "woes" by which Christ expressed his deep anger at religious leaders of the day).

Anger as Care

Angry, hurting people are often people who care. Behind the intensity of passion of anger is the emotion of passionate care. People who are aroused by injustice and abuse are people who care. There is no passion where people are not deeply invested. To understand the rage of anger is to appreciate the significance of our sense of justice. Made in the image of God, we are hopefully alert to our own value as human beings and to the importance of just treatment for ourselves and others (Genesis 1:26-28).

Jesus obviously appreciated the anger of the abused, because he himself responded with anger to those who abused. He felt strongly about the oppressed and those unjustly treated; he himself was both abused and ill-treated. He warned his followers of the injustice and manipulation of people (Matthew 5:11-12). He joined the oppressed in angrily denouncing the injustices of his day (Matthew 23:13-33, Mark 3:5, Luke 13:15, John 2:13-17). Like the God of Israel, incensed by Israel's carelessness and abuse, Jesus wept passionately over the insensitivity of his local community (Luke 13:34ff).

The Right to Be Angry: A Blessing

Abused people often struggle to give themselves permission to feel anger. Taught as Christians to place ourselves last in line to respond to our own needs, we frequently resist the notion that we deserve to be cared for when we are neglected, abused, or manipulated. We need to give ourselves the same permission that God and Jesus Christ taught us in the Scriptures. We need to acknowledge that it is appropriate and normal to feel anger when abused, neglected, or used. God expressed deep anger at Israel and anyone else who misused their relationship. Jesus Christ displayed passionate anger at those who carelessly abused others (Mark 8:33).

It is not easy to express an internal rage and a deep sense of injustice. We probably first shed tears because we have no adequate vocabulary for the pain and stress within us. But the anguish and frustration of those who have been ill-treated needs recognition and expression beyond tears. Finding the words and feelings to express that experience is our first challenge.

Understanding the value and validity of our anger is probably the first step toward healing tears of anger. Kathryn needed someone who would give her permission to feel her anger for what it was and to "bless" its expression. Our initial attempts to express our emotions may be awkward and difficult, but our tears may lead us to the first release of feelings—and to a clearer understanding of our underlying passion for what is right. Such moments are intense and painful; they are also holy ground.

To get permission to discover the source of our anger, we need a friend or confidant who accepts, and is interested in, the feelings behind the tears. Such a person helps us by making clear that the intensity of our feelings will not upset them. When we have suppressed important emotions for a long time, it is natural to feel frightened about the intensity of the passion inside of us. We fear losing control or that we will embarrass ourselves or that our pain will overwhelm others.

That is why caring for someone who is angry involves a calm, steady, listening presence. Kathryn needed me to listen attentively to her. She needed someone who would receive her tears as important and listen to the anger behind them. The faithful, calm willingness to sit by someone in the throes of passionate anger is one of the best healing gifts we can offer. People need to know that we are not afraid of their feelings and that their expression will neither hurt us, nor them.

Finding someone who will accept and receive our anger is good news. There is a vital redemptive function in having a witness to our tears of outrage. The silent companionship of a caring other gives us courage to face the hurt inside.

Uncovering our anger in our fearful journey is a sacred moment that confirms the value of our tears. Our angry tears become unexpected but significant friends, helping us identify important feelings as we try to "speak our mind." With the psalmist, we need to give ourselves permission to cry out:

> My God, my God, why have you forsaken me?
> Why are you so far from saving me,
> so far from the words of my groaning?
> O my God, I cry out by day, but you do not answer,
> by night, and am not silent. (Psalm 22:1-2)

The passionate anger of those who feel abandoned, betrayed, or wronged, needs to be expressed. Expressing this inner pain is a cleansing function reserved for those who grasp the sacred hem of some invisible divine garment and plead for vindication in an unjust world.

I was a priestly witness to that cry from Kathryn; anyone who chooses to care, and finds himself or herself elected to such trust, can do the same. Our tearful language does not require many words of response. We are looking in a crowd of faces for a caring glance. The redemptive gifts we offer, if we choose to give them, are a look of recognition, a validating phrase, and an initial assurance. Wounded as we are, such acknowledgments assure us that someone else knows our passion, understands our anger, and cares about the vulnerable people this careless world uses and ignores.

Our Anger and God: Who Is to Blame?

Angry Christians often struggle with their feelings toward God. Where was God when we were injured? If God is good, why does the Almighty not intervene when pain and evil occur? Where is God when we ask for relief from our pain? Friends who mean well sometimes feel the need to "defend" God if anyone raises questions that challenge either God's goodness or interest in us. The truth is that God can handle any of our questions, all our confusion, and all our anger. The Scriptures remind us of how often human beings questioned or "blessed" God and survived (Psalm 22:1, Psalm 142:1, Job 4:1-2, etc.).

People who are angry need the freedom to express their deep emotions without fear of judgment. The challenge of abuse and injustice is that we frequently don't know where to take our complaint. Like the early Hebrews, our childhood "contract" with God may have been that no harm would come to us if we faithfully believed and followed. When "bad things happen to good people," then, we may join the suffering Job of the Old Testament in wondering where God is when injustice and suffering happen to us (Job 7).

Abuse and injustice are stunning reminders that God's will is not always done in this world. Those of us who experience human irresponsibility, manipulation, and abuse are immediately aware that human beings have the power to hurt and destroy, and that all of us have the freedom to act in ways contrary to God's intention.

The very first chapter of the Bible describes a loving God who chooses to make us in the image of love — and therefore will not make robots of us.

Such freedom requires that we be endowed with a will of our own, so that we may choose to love. Love is never coercive and will not impose its will over another. The God in whose image we have been made gave the entire creation freedom to follow or ignore the Maker's will. As human beings, we choose how we will act, think, and live. The story of the first murder recorded in Scripture is a parable of our capacity to choose to harm rather than help (Genesis 1:26-28, 4:8-10).

Our first encounter with personal injury may force us to reexamine our understanding of how God works in an imperfect world. At first we may feel angry at God for not preventing evil and chaos. We may struggle with God's decision to give all of us the power to choose between good and evil. We may wish that God had protected us from injustice — or we may flinch at the pain of abuse, as Jesus Christ did from the cross (Psalm 22:1, Matthew 27:46). We may learn in that same scene at Golgotha that God neither promised to protect nor shielded his own son from harm.

We have the right to tell God that this fallible world is often a painful, abusive, and unfair place. We have the right to tell God when we are hurting from oppression, neglect, and manipulation. God has not promised us that we can avoid abuse or pain; God has promised us that we will never be abandoned in this cruel world — and that beyond this world of time and space God's will and way will one day preside — and never be abolished. Our promise is that one day when God reigns there will be no more sadness, death, pain, or tears . . . (Revelation 21:4).

Meanwhile, in this fragile, fickle life, our tear-filled anger is our solemn, wrenching prayer, which rises as a true complaint to God. Unjustly treated, we struggle to be faithful and seek some sign in the silence, which denies that we have been abandoned or ignored by God. Those of us who are privileged to bear witness to these outcries of the soul may also in the process become faithful, humble, and caring reminders of a loving and compassionate God who walks with each wounded person through the valley of the shadows. The God of Jesus Christ is then a friend who gives no easy answers, offers no quick exits, and promises no painless journeys, but provides the courage of companionship in some of our journey's darkest moments.

Thus the gospel of hope emerges during tears of anger. Through such a response, manipulation, abuse, and tragedy are not ignored, sidestepped, nor minimized. Rather, the gentle, steady, nonjudgmental reception of deep anger assures us that our anguish is legitimate, that our feelings are to be taken seriously, and that voicing those feelings will neither overwhelm us nor separate us from the love of God and the community of friends (Romans 8:35-9).

Protecting the Vulnerable

When we have been abused, we feel invaded and vulnerable. We not only need validation of our feelings, but a strategy for healing and self-protection. Abused persons have a fragile sense of security once they have been violated. We need help protecting ourselves from oppressors of all kinds. We need to make sure that we are no longer as vulnerable as we were when we were exploited. Kathryn, for example, needed to take measures to insure her personal safety.

For Kathryn, examining her own safety meant looking carefully at her schedule, living quarters, and daily habits in order to minimize the possibility of another attack. Her fear of being beaten again made it almost impossible for her to name her attacker. As long as we surrender such power to an abuser, we are at their mercy.

I tried to get Kathryn's permission to engage the police as a witness to her physical condition and as a legal ally in her struggle to protect herself from this law student's abuse. She was so afraid of him that at first she was only agreeable to measures which would make her less accessible to her attacker's inappropriate (and illegal) behavior. Unfortunately, a common practice among abusers is to choose victims whose self-esteem is so low that they do not value themselves as human beings and allow repeated violent incidents before asking for protection.

Regaining Perspective

There are many tears the angry person must cry. Competent and effective care of victims of injustice requires patience, understanding, and compassion. Unless we have been through a similar tragedy before, we may underestimate the power of manipulation. We need to be patient with our need to cry out when abused, and to understand the depth and extent of our agony over being violated.

Compassionate, gradual healing begins to occur when we admit our anger and become willing to release the rage accumulated over being wronged. Friends help us most by not pretending to understand how we feel. Honest comments are more valuable than the glib sentiment of someone trying to manage their own anxiety.

Our tears and anger flow from the profound anguish of having lost faith in humanity. We are also dealing with the fact that a violent event has changed us: we are no longer who we were. We have been permanently affected. We shed the bitter tears of disappointment and anger because we have no control over what has been. We face our pain and sorrow—a courageous act—and begin the healing process. We come to terms with the agony of an injustice that cannot be retracted. We struggle with the fact that we cannot undo what has been done—only recover from it and refuse to be controlled by it.

Recovery and Renewal

The gradual healing of angered, misused persons is a long process. Central to its occurrence is the necessity of dealing with our anger in an accepting, redemptive way. To acknowledge and process the passion of anger is to recognize our value as a person who deserves responsible treatment. Such understanding recognizes our anger as a measure of our belief in our worth and purpose. Our anger also validates the need to take ourselves seriously, so that we can be released from the injustice of an event and make our future manageable. Acknowledging angry tears helps us understand the nature of our passion. Such recognition allows distressed persons to focus on the reality of their loss, the frustration of the unchangeable, the legitimate need to protest its injury, and eventually to determine what we can control—our future.

The work of care involves patient hours of "talking out" our rage. A faithful witness who listens allows the wronged griever to come to terms with the reality of the unchangeable. Gradually the realization that "life goes on whether it's fair or not" begins to take hold. As one preacher puts it, the angered soul needs "a witness here" to verify the wrong. Like Job seeking a friend who will testify to our injury, we need someone who will stand and say, "You were wronged!"

Anger at Ourselves: Injury?

Sometimes we turn our unfocused rage on ourselves. Angry tears become punitive tears and we begin to blame ourselves for what happened. We tell ourselves that if we had been more cautious, or smarter, or more skillful, we could have avoided the painful event. We begin to question whether we inadvertently encouraged the intrusion—either by some behavior or word. Angry that we have been injured, we turn on the easiest victim to blame: ourselves.

Somewhere in such conversations we may struggle with the notion of hurting ourselves or even killing ourselves to stop the pain. Suicidal thoughts are not uncommon with those who have been abused or wronged. Feeling mistreated, we want to punish in return. Battling self-hatred, we turn our anger inside.

Self-destructive thinking and behavior during such episodes needs immediate attention. When we hate ourselves, we usually become depressed, lose interest in things that used to attract us, rehearse self-blaming and destructive thoughts, and wonder what it would be like to put an end to our pain. Such anger is misplaced and damaging. We have already been punished enough in the event that harmed us. If suicidal or self-destructive thoughts crowd our mind, we need help.

Rape victims, who frequently blame themselves for a violent crime they did not initiate, sometimes need to be reminded that they are the victims of a violent, angry act—not a sexual activity. Because rape is disguised as a sexual encounter, it is frequently misunderstood as a sexual act. Rape is a physical assault with intent to distress another. Victims of rape and other violent, destructive behaviors need special care for their recovery. When we are victimized in such a way, we need healing physically, emotionally, and spiritually. Rape crises centers and other caring agencies are best equipped to handle the severe trauma of sexual assault.

People who are angry at themselves need care in identifying their misplaced pain. When we hurt badly enough to want to kill ourselves, we need to reach out and ask for help, because we have lost perspective. Asking for help is a way of making sure that someone else will protect us and save us from the waste of suicide. Medication and rest are two important ways to gain perspective—and usually keep us from making a poor decision about our life. Sometimes we are hurting too much to know what's best for us. A trusted friend, minister, family member, or caring hospital medic can help.

Anger need not become our enemy. No injustice in the world should rob us of our right to live. Teresa Saldana, a television and movie star who was sexually abused, reminded us of that in her autobiography, *Beyond Survival.* Struggling to find meaning for her life after a savage assault almost took her life, she agonized with self-anger and wrestled with hopelessness. In the painful months of physical recovery, she came to the conclusion that she was not going to allow anything that had happened to her rob her of her future. She determined that she had no control over what had happened in her past, but that she could control her future.

Learning to embrace our pain teaches us that our anger and hurt will not control us. As we slowly learn to manage our pain, we discover not only that we will survive, but that we can regain control. And when we understand that we will gradually regain focus and control, we learn to give ourselves permission to be patient with our wounds as they heal.

First we will probably discover our capacity to return to our routine. Then we will notice that we are slowly coping better. Eventually we will reawaken some passion and interest in our day and week. Peace of mind and joy will begin to reappear. Confidence will increase its foothold.

The first evidence of hope is a return to routine without enthusiasm or joy. The structure of a schedule can greatly assist people looking for a place to stand after life has caved in. Even a few mechanical routines can provide us with the first glimpse of stability and recovery. Anguished victims of tragedy sometimes need to be reassured that returning to simple tasks is not a sign that the agony is over. The first steps of re-entry are small ones, but balance and routines bring security. The distraught and angry person needs to set small and "do-able" goals for self-care and reentry. Returning to a working schedule is a victory.

Tears of anger may return without warning. In the middle of the day, during a distracted moment, or in the midst of a happy memory, a sudden reminder of our anguish returns with all its contrast. The recurring memory is triggered by the depth of our wound and the reminder that our life has been altered and will not be the same again. But these stunning reminders will gradually give way to longer periods of reflection, acceptance, and peace. Painful moments gradually subside.

We may need to remind ourselves periodically that bitter tears and painful memories are solid steps on the journey toward recovery. To understand anger and agony in tears is to understand the language of the human heart. The psalmist often described such anguish as a "lamentation." The lamenting believer writes and sings repeatedly of her pain, and in so doing disposes of her anguish in a repetitive "emptying" of her bitter cup.

What is the nature of angry tears? Such tears are the passionate language of a life that has been scarred. Angry tears are the poignant cry of persons who have unfairly lost something very precious and have no way of recovering the loss. The tears of anger are the exasperated vocabulary we summon when we have no words to say what we feel, how much we have lost, or how strongly we hurt over being wronged. Like the psalmist, we plead:

> Turn to me and be gracious to me, for I am lonely and afflicted. The troubles of my heart have multiplied; free me from my anguish. Look upon my affliction and my distress . . . (Psalm 25:16-18).

Chapter 2

———— ◆ ————

Tears of Confession

You do not delight in sacrifice, or I would bring it;
You do not take pleasure in burnt offerings.
The sacrifices of God are a broken spirit;
a broken and contrite heart,
O God, you will not despise.
—Psalm 51: 16-17

MARY CALLED FOR AN APPOINTMENT and told me that she "just needed to get some things off her mind." When I met her at the office door, she entered quietly, barely maintaining a forced smile. By the time she reached a chair, she was overcome with tears.

I waited quietly for a few minutes, aware that sometimes we interrupt a vital process when we talk during the early flow of tears. I noticed her struggle to control the crying and said, "Take your time. There's a lot of feeling in your tears and there's no hurry."

Mary's crying continued for a few minutes, and then she interrupted her tears with an apology: "I'm so sorry . . . I promised myself I wouldn't do this in here, but I guess I've been crying off and on for two weeks now. I'm not surprised . . . I can't seem to stop." I assured her that her tears were a gesture of trust and that she could share whatever she was feeling. She seemed to relax and gave me an account of her struggle.

She had been romantically involved with another student at the university and, after a squabble, had returned home for the weekend to see a former boyfriend. Over the weekend, Mary and her former boyfriend had become sexually involved. Returning to school, she found herself unable to sleep at night. She was seeing me after five sleepless nights.

"I guess I just needed to tell somebody . . . I'm not sure why I came her . . . I just felt the need to talk about it with someone . . . I can't tell my folks — I don't want my boyfriend here to know . . . There is a friend I've told . . . But I can't stop crying and I can't get it off my mind."

Sensing that some interpretation might help her better understand her struggle, I mentioned that when we grieve and wrestle with guilt we usually are confused by the variety of feelings. The recurring bouts of sudden tears and the painful cycle of depressive thoughts and feelings are especially disturbing.

"We go through so many feelings when we're confused about something, Mary. It sounds like you're struggling with mixed feelings over what happened. Are you aware of particular thoughts or feelings?" I phrased the question sitting in my pastor's study, across the street from a major private university where many students came from strong, conservative religious homes.

"There is a lot of pain in your face, and your tears are steady," I continued. "Sometimes tears are our way of forcing out the pain inside because it's bothering us." She nods and looks steadily at me, apparently agreeing with my comment. "It seems to be really working on you night and day. You've had little sleep, restless thoughts, and heavy feelings. Anything else?"

Her tears started, then stopped as Mary focused on what I was saying. She nodded and asked, "How do I get past all this? So much of what you just said is how I've been feeling for three days now! I can't seem to get past it."

"There are powerful feelings inside of us," I said, "and it takes a little time to work them out. Feelings don't just leave when we tell them to leave." Mary began to cry again. "But if you can identify the cause of your pain, then you're on your way to relief and healing. I'll be glad to help you sift through some of the confusion and see if we can find out what has you hurting inside."

Mary was still crying, although a little softer, and she tried to talk. "I think I need to start right away. I don't think I'll sleep much until I do. How do I start?"

"You already have," I replied. "The moment you walked into the room, you were on your way. Thanks for trusting me with your pain. Tell me what you think is bothering you."

Mary's struggle came from her confusion about feelings of guilt and shame for her weekend behavior. She had no idea how to identify her feelings and, at first, was quite surprised that her feelings were those of guilt. But a lifetime of religious guidance on responsible sexual behavior is not easily set aside; inside she was fighting a battle between what she felt she believed—and what she had done. Her first words in the struggle were in the language of tears.

*   *   *   *   *

People inside and outside of the church have always needed to confess. Along with our need to be affirmed and loved, we also have deep needs for confession, atonement, and reconciliation:

> For I know my transgressions,
> and my sin is always before me.
> Against you, you only, have I sinned
> and done what is evil in your sight . . . (Psalm 51:3-4).

The Power of Guilt and Shame

Almost all of us have grown up in a society and a family with standards of conduct. Our ideas on how to treat others are reinforced by important codes we learn to value in religious circles. We have learned some distinctions between what we consider right and wrong, and we have developed certain values about how we want to be treated—and how we should treat others. When we disappoint ourselves or others, we struggle with guilt, shame, or both.

Guilt, remorse, and shame, like toxic waste, need to be properly processed. We need some way to work through or dispose of these feelings. Whether we have done "wrong" or not, our perception of failing our own standards, or those of others, can weigh heavily on us. Taking responsibility for a wrong we believe we've caused is a major step in processing emotional pain. Through confession, we can lift the burden of our pain and self-condemnation. The very act of sharing unburdens us of carrying our pain alone. And when we confess, we summon forgiveness from someone. This forgiveness reduces our anxiety and our sense of worthlessness. It restores our self-esteem and peace.

When we break rules and principles we believe in, we also suffer what some people call "moral pain." The anguish of moral pain needs resolution and healing, and our capacity to confess has a lot to do with our ability to heal. When we know we've done something which goes against what we believe, we react with intense self-criticism. Our borrowed and accepted standards of behavior are very important to us, and any violation of them affects us deeply. The intense pain churning inside us often expresses itself in bitter tears. We feel alienated from ourselves until we confess.

When we identify behaviors or actions that we condemn, we can voice them and take responsibility for them. When we voice such experiences, we become "confessors" and begin to dispose of our moral pain. The very act of voicing expels the tension we have stored inside of us. The act of trusting another human being with the content of our inner pain is healing. Counselors and ministers have known for years that the process of naming our struggles can reduce the tension inside us. The additional power of having our private pain received by another is therapeutic; it restores peace by calming our restless mind and heart.

Precisely because confession has a healing effect, several religious groups provide ways for confessing, for channeling self-condemnation and pain. Some of us, however, grew up in traditions that offered no clear way of acknowledging failures and mistakes. Without ways to identify and process personal wrongs, we struggle to gain freedom from it. Tears of confession are often the first sign that we are burdened by deep inner discomfort, remorse, and self-condemnation.

There is no doubt that moral pain and guilt often struggle for a voice. Consider the Vietnam veteran, struggling to hold back his tears, as he talks about following orders that required him to kill men, women, and children living in a suspected Vietcong village. He recalls the agony of pointing his rifle at civilians—total strangers to him—and then killing everyone in sight—the contrary of everything he had been taught growing up. He remembers the unusual brutality and violence of those moments, and he strains to put into words how he felt then—and how he feels now. His outreach coordinator declares: "We aren't just counselors to them. We're like priests and they are coming to us for absolution."

Whether we belong to a religious group or not, all of us need such priests. When we struggle with internal condemnation, we look for someone who will help us deal with our guilt, shame, or remorse. We need to tell someone our faults, and we hope they will help us dispose of them. So we bring our saddest memories, often clothed in tears, and deposit them in faith at the feet of a chosen "priest." We hope that this universal language of tears will interpret our voiceless heart, and start a conversation that will release us from our pain.

Feelings are often deep rivers that contain important issues. Tears are sometimes the means by which our soul tries to "speak" to another. Tears of confession are, sometimes, the first clue that we are troubled by moral pain; tears often help us start vital conversations.

Tears of confession do not release us from the burden of our struggle. They were only meant to help us start the journey of release. Tears alone do not heal confessors; they permit us to come to terms with acts and thoughts we regret. We must then travel through particular experiences and their pain before we can feel forgiven and released. We must come to terms with our own failure to do right. We must acknowledge our pain and express our regret. We must, therefore, identify the struggle behind our tears.

Whoever said, "Confession is good for the soul," was right. The act of telling someone else what we have done takes away some of the pain and weight we have carried. We need a way to state our sense of failure. Acknowledging our mistakes means we take responsibility for them; it also means we are sorry and asking forgiveness for our mistakes.

All we can do sometimes is acknowledge the wrong, because some things cannot be repaired. David, king of Israel, wept bitter tears at the news of his son Absalom's death. The king had failed to act when his family and his son had needed him; no tears would bring him back (2 Samuel 18).

At other times, we voice our inner pain as a way of "coming clean" with our past. The prisoner of war guard who weeps confessionally as he recalls his irresponsible behavior years before, seeks with his tears to confess, to somehow "pay" for his crime. Religious groups call such efforts "atoning." This atonement is a way to be released from our "moral debt."

Steps in Confession

How do we gain help for our tears of confession? We begin by finding the courage to talk about the turmoil inside us. We seek out a trusted "receiver" who will listen responsibly to our pain and guilt. Next, we try to identify the issues, behaviors, or memories that haunt us. Then we take responsibility for our actions and behaviors. We discover how to accept forgiveness for things we cannot change. Finally, we learn to let go of paralyzing memories and take hold of what we can do—shape our future.

1. Finding the courage to talk: It is very hard to tell someone else about our pain. It is also very hard on us not to talk about our inner turmoil. Few of us seem to realize how much energy it takes to contain our feelings. Keeping secrets is hard on us because we review our pain constantly. We sometimes feel exhausted from carrying a problem because it takes a significant amount of energy to "manage" a troubling issue by ourselves.

Should this person I'm talking with know this much about me? Is it actually necessary for me to tell anyone what has happened? The struggle within us between two opposing needs is evident. There is a part of us that wants to reveal and be known, a part that wants to hide and remain closed.

Perhaps the most compelling argument for sharing our struggle, however, is the persistent pain we weather until we do share it. In Mary's case the sleepless, difficult nights prompted her to seek relief. For some of us, it is the restless, gnawing discomfort deep inside, and the unpredictable tears that surprise us on every turn—and haunt us until we find help. The price for not speaking is far greater than the price for voicing our strain. The sooner we realize the expensive, hidden toll we pay for not expressing our hurt, the sooner we will seek someone out. Medical clinics are filled with depressed people who punish themselves by swallowing their guilt, and with wounded people who literally make themselves sick before they give voice to their inner turmoil.

2. Finding a responsible listener: Choosing a confessor is an important task. All of us have been ridiculed, rejected, or betrayed at some time. Our greatest fear in telling someone our secret is that we will be abused. When confessing, most of us initially look for a person we can trust, a person who is accepting, attentive, and non-judgmental. We look for someone who will understand, who will know how to care for us, and who will help us.

For some of us, our best friend is our first confidant. But many of us still seek out a minister first, probably because ministers are accessible and caring. For others, it may be a counselor, a social worker, or a doctor. The most important thing is to find someone with whom we can safely share our inner self.

If, as confessors, we suspect that we are being negatively received at the start of the conversation, we may need to ask our confidant for clarification. If negative signals continue, we may need to excuse ourselves as quickly and gracefully as possible. As confessors, we need responsible listeners who will also protect our confidentiality. We need people with whom we feel secure; we want others who will stand by us regardless of what we say. We want friends; we need advocates. We need people skilled enough to realize what a powerful gift we offer them when we share our private selves. We also need those who can help us receive our feelings, manage our pain, and give us hope.

Be alert for friends who are too eager to forgive. Sometimes listeners dispense grace too early, before we are ready to receive it. All of us need time to process our guilt and sort out our feelings. We want our faults taken seriously, and we don't want to be pronounced whole or forgiven until we have completed our struggles.

On the other hand, a "rush to judgment" may also occur. Those of us who confess may have encountered a few clergy or other caregivers with rigid moral injunctions who mistakenly believe they need to quickly condemn our revelations, perhaps out of fear that they will be perceived as condoning particular behaviors. We may find ourselves stunned by their strong reactions.

Such listeners mistake a confessional conversation for a time to "set people straight." What they don't understand is that we who come to confess are already aware of our failures and mistakes; we don't need an additional judgment leveled on us— we've already done that ourselves. We need people to listen to our moral pain and our self-condemnation; those who can offer us hope of forgiveness and hope that we can get past our mistakes.

If we cry during our first difficult moments in confession, we need people who understand our need to cry, who are sensitive to our fear of self-disclosure. We need those who can be patient with us while we sort out our thoughts and feelings.

We may struggle to understand what we want to say. Being anxious is a natural beginning to such important disclosures. As we settle down and focus, fear and anxiety will diminish. People who care and understand know how to put us at ease, and are interested in letting us find our pace.

3. Identifying the issue: The more clearly we can declare our reason for this visit, the easier we can get to what is on our mind. "I came to you because I trust you and because I'm hurting; because I need you to help me sort my feelings." If we can be clear, we can offer our chosen listeners an invitation to our stories and struggles.

This is no time for casual conversation. The sooner we begin to talk about what is bothering us, the more at ease we will be. Every caregiver I know is grateful for direction from us and eager to move with us into our place of need. A carefully chosen priest is willing and equipped to move into deeper waters.

We need not worry about organizing our thoughts. We may fear that we are rambling, but once we've started talking, our shared thoughts will make sense and become clear. Trained listeners know how to ask us questions and elicit clarity; our job is mainly to share what is on our mind. Chances are, we have rehearsed our concerns enough in our own minds, so that the important center of our confession should unfold without confusion.

Rarely does someone choose a confessor and not share. Naturally, we share part of our story and wait to see how it's treated. If our gift is taken seriously and our sincerity honored, we will choose to say more. We always have the right to choose how much to share and when to stop. We may also choose the time when we feel right and ready for confidential disclosures.

One final word about confession: as we begin to tell our story, several elements may seem important. Comments may cascade one upon the other. Clarity may seem to be missing. But more than likely we will provide all the necessary details. Anxious as we may be, we may fear that we are incoherent, but that is rarely the case. If we cry when telling our stories, let the tears weave themselves into the conversation, for they are integral to expressing our deepest needs.

If there are several issues to discuss, let the issues come as they will. A good listener will help us discern which concerns bear the greatest pain. On the other hand, if we haven't identified exactly what is troubling us, a simple retelling of our stories will help us focus on issues.

4. Clarifying and claiming what is ours: A crucial issue in the resolution of guilt and shame is clarifying responsibility. We sometimes feel guilt about behaviors for which we are responsible. Sometimes we assume responsibility for things beyond our control. In the book (and movie) *Schindler's List*, the main figure, a Czech businessman named Schindler, realizes the plight of Jews he had employed in Poland, so he buys the release of over eight hundred Jews bound for death camps and then cries bitterly for having squandered money that could have "bought" several more lives. He spends a fortune to save over eight hundred people; yet, he still feels guilt.

Victims of sexual abuse commonly feel responsible for the violence perpetrated on them. Some people in our society still suggest that rape victims bring their own problems. It is important, therefore, that we assess with someone else the reality of our guilt or shame. Some of us need to learn we cannot take responsibility for all things that happen.

When we have done wrong or sinned, confession becomes our road to accepting responsibility for our faults and to taking our mistakes seriously. In everyday conversation, we may ask if he owned up to it. What we are really asking is whether he took responsibility for his behavior. Confession gives us that opportunity. David took such responsibility for his inappropriate behavior toward Bathsheba and Uriah (2 Samuel): "For I know my transgressions, and my sin is ever before me . . ." (Psalm 51:3). We, too, can confront our faults, and admit them.

The act of acknowledging our irresponsible behavior begins the releasing process. Guilt and shame are eased. The groundwork is established for potential forgiveness.

5. Anxiety during confession: Initial moments in confession are significant. A sensitive listener will give us quiet reassurance and privacy at that time. We should feel that what we say is safe and confidential.

This is no time for trivial conversation. We are opening the curtain that conceals our souls. Hopefully we and our listener understand that we are entering "holy ground." We note signals in the conversation: Is there a tone of rejection in the listener's voice? Is there an early hint of judgment? Is there a silence that suggests condemnation—or disinterest? We read facial expressions, verbal pauses, and "body language" for clues about how our disclosures are received. Giving birth to a confession is very hard. Fear of condemnation makes us especially alert to rejection.

An alert, quiet response often indicates that our priest is taking us seriously and trying to follow our words. Silence is not condemnation; these moments are ours to express anything we want to say and we need not feel rushed nor distracted. Perhaps we have waited a long time for someone we could trust.

Accepting Forgiveness

Some people do not wish to be forgiven. We may come to ministers looking for grace, but believe that we cannot or should not be forgiven. Most of us who struggle with forgiveness are unprepared to forgive ourselves. Our capacity to receive forgiveness may depend on our understanding of resistance in confession.

Why do we resist forgiveness? Sometimes we have trouble believing that God can forgive us; or sometimes we understand that God can forgive, but doubt that our friends or family can forgive. Sometimes we cannot forgive ourselves. For each of these struggles, the Scriptures give helpful instruction and offer hope and grace.

Students of the Scriptures remind us that "sin against the Holy Spirit" is one in which the activity and work of God's spirit in our life is blunted by our refusal to allow the spirit of God to work in us. Obviously, control over the Spirit's work is clearly in our hands, not God's. We and not God, therefore, are responsible for allowing the grace of God into our lives.

If we are struggling with the boundaries under which God's spirit can work (and forgive), we need to understand that we ourselves set the boundaries (and the limitations) for grace, not God. All of us have the power to set limits on God's grace by not allowing it to be active in our lives. The scriptural truth is that we have asked the wrong question. It is not "What can't God forgive?" but "Where have I placed limits on God's grace in my life?"

This rewording is not a word game, but a very important distinction: I can resist God's grace in my life by not allowing myself to receive God's presence and healing. For confessors, this truth means that they should pay attention to the limits they place on God's grace. The boundaries of forgiveness are not drawn by God, but by us—and we can remove them.

When we fear that others will not forgive us, we may simply need to talk with those we fear are rejecting us. If we find it hard to start such conversations, ministers and other caregivers can help bring us together and see that such conversations take place.

It may be helpful to ask ourselves, "Who am I afraid will not forgive me?" Usually there are only one or two persons on such lists. The fact that we fear the rejection of only one or two may be a source of relief in itself.

In some cases we may have good reasons to fear rejection. There are persons who do reject, judge, and condemn. A careful evaluation with our counselors can help us assess how likely certain persons are to reject us—and whether some conversations will only yield unnecessary pain and condemnation. In that case, we may want further help in rehearsing our best possible options.

One of our greatest fears is that people will not release us through forgiveness. Behind such fear is our awareness that some people like to control us by deliberately withholding grace. They seek power over us. They want to hold our mistakes over our heads. Redemptive confessing on our part provides us an opportunity to find release from our failings—even when some people will not forgive us. How does this work?

Our biblical models are useful again: When Jesus encounters a crowd prepared to stone a woman for her sexual irresponsibility, he confronts them with their own sins and then asks the innocent to be the first to condemn (John 7). He then turns to the woman, charges her with responsibility for her future, and releases her. We may need to accept God's grace — even when others choose not to forgive us. When we have confessed and asked for forgiveness, we need to release ourselves (as God does) from the paralysis of not living by grace, even though some misguided person will not "bless us" with forgiveness.

If we feel unforgiven, we may need to be reminded that God forgives us and releases us to new opportunities daily, just as Israel experienced with the Lord of hope. Just as God did not withhold grace from Israel, so we are forgiven and set free. Psalm 103:10-12 says:

> [God] does not treat us as our sins deserve or repay us according our iniquities. For as high as the heavens are above the earth, so great is his love for those who fear him; as far as the east is from the west, so far has he removed our transgressions from us.

To be dependent on the forgiveness of others in order to be released from our past is to leave us in other people's control. When people are unwilling to forgive and release, we must claim God's grace for ourselves and live unshackled by the past.

The Apostle Luke writes: "The Spirit of the Lord . . . has sent me to proclaim freedom for the prisoners . . . to release the oppressed . . ." (Luke 4:18). We are pronounced forgiven, not in our name, but in the name and nature of the one who forgave Israel and sent Jesus Christ to release us.

Often we say that God cannot forgive us, when the problem is we cannot forgive ourselves. We often are hard on ourselves. It is not surprising, therefore, that most people find it easier to forgive others than to forgive themselves.

Part of our struggle is that we know ourselves well. We understand our mixed motives and our imperfect thoughts. We know we are inconsistent, even fickle. How can we forgive ourselves? We can do so only if we understand that everyone else is just like us, and that God responded with grace to an unstable and regularly inconsistent set of followers in the Scriptures. A brief study of Abraham, Jacob, Moses, David, and others will remind us that God works always with very imperfect people.

Christ reminds us that he knows his sheep, and that he loves even those who betray him. The power of Christ's forgiveness is felt both at a table, where his best friends confess they had all considered betraying him (Mark 14), and on the cross, when he asks the Father to forgive his crucifiers because they did not understand what they were doing (Luke 23).

When we think our sins are greater than those of others, we need to be reminded of the sins his followers were forgiven: murder, infidelity, betrayal, denial, doubt, greed, and selfishness. We also need to remember that Christ sought out Peter to forgive and release him after Peter's betrayal. The fact is that Judas and Peter were both guilty of the same offense. Judas could not forgive himself. Peter struggled through remorse and confession, progressing to grace and restitution.

When we resist forgiveness, we may be unintentionally challenging God by suggesting that we understand the nature of our sin better than God. Such awkward posturing can imply that we believe God does not understand the nature of sin, forgiveness, and grace in our lives.

Atonement: How We Pay

In the absence of a clear plan for paying our debts, we sometimes create our own atonement plans. Such plans can become a condition of our release from guilt.

People who cry the tears of confession often need tangible ways to atone. Some religious organizations (the Roman Catholic Church, for example, in its rite of confession) have clear directions for behaviors that express contrition for transgressors. Forgiveness, then, is clearly attained when the confessor performs certain acts and a priest pronounces forgiveness.

We, too, may be searching for a way to find peace of mind and release. In some cases, we can receive forgiveness by hearing words of forgiveness from those to whom we confess. We sometimes empower clergy and other members of religious orders with the authority to pronounce us forgiven because we accept their role as representatives of God.

A simple, straightforward statement that God forgives us may be all some of us need in order to be released from our struggle. But some of us may be looking for a tangible way of atoning. We are looking for a concrete act (for example, acts of charity) that we might perform to make amends for our behavior. Our answer may be a specified number of hours volunteering our services to some worthy cause. Sometimes I've suggested that an anonymous act of service be performed daily for a certain number of days, as a way of providing concrete actions for those of us who need to "do" good to repair any harm we feel we've caused.

In some traditions, prayers and fasting have been used for centuries as tangible expressions of contrition and repair. Some believers find it helpful to deprive themselves of particular things for certain periods of time. Each of us is unique. We may need to help our listeners by suggesting actions that are meaningful to us as a means of apprehending grace and embracing "newness of life."

Several religious groups use prayers that remind all of us that God is not in the business of punishment and rejection, but in the daily work of grace and responsible freedom. Whatever words or behaviors help us take hold of God's gifts of grace and hope should be freely and joyfully employed. We are, after all, seeking the "peace that passes understanding" (Philippians 4), and a place where our tears of confession will give way to a new way of living:

> [God] will wipe every tear from their eyes. There shall be no more death or mourning or crying or pain, for the old order of things has passed away (Revelation 21:4).

Where Do We Go From Here?

Christ's powerful gift to sinners is his understanding that they are more important than their sins. Unlike the Pharisees, who Christ criticized for valuing the rules more than the people for whom the rules were made, Jesus clearly let it be known that the people were more important than the rules he followed. He believed that people were not made for the sabbath (the rules) but that the sabbath was made for the sake of the people. Hence Paul's great affirmation:

> For I am convinced that neither death, nor life . . . nor anything else in all creation, will be able to separate us from the love of God that is in Christ Jesus our Lord (Romans 8:38-39).

If we are to find hope, we need to receive grace. We have raised some important questions in order to reach that hopeful place. Confession is an important means of taking our mistakes seriously, yet not letting them permanently cripple us or rob us of a joyous future. Those who help us in our confession by their willingness to receive our voiced sins become instruments of God's grace and hope for us. We trust these messengers of grace because they understand our tears even before we can speak. In this way, tears of confession, properly understood, become our doorway to freedom from paralyzing guilt.

Chapter 3

———— ◆ ————

Tears of Failure

My eyes are full of tears
because my heart is full —
My heart is full
Because it harbors my defeat. . . .

H E AWOKE THAT NIGHT to the agitated cries of his
mother. She was yelling for him because his dad had
apparently had a heart attack and had stopped breathing.
While his mother called for help, the twelve-year old was
pressed into service to give his father artificial respiration
until the paramedics could arrive. He tried as best he could.
When the paramedics arrived, however, they pronounced
his father dead. An adult now, his cheeks still flush when he
recalls that moment and remembers the tears — and the
haunting feeling of having failed.

Few experiences are more discouraging than the recognition that we have failed. We fear failing in relationships, in
personal goals, and in realizing our potential as people.
Agony comes upon us when all our efforts fail — when we feel
defeated. Peter, one of the most promising disciples, reminds
us of how vulnerable we all are to the misery of failing a
friend:

About an hour later another asserted, "Certainly this fellow was with him, for he is a Galilean."

Peter replied, "Man, I don't know what you're talking about!" Just as he was speaking, the rooster crowed. The Lord turned and looked straight at Peter. Then Peter remembered the word the Lord had spoken to him: "Before the rooster crows today, you will disown me three times." And he went outside and wept bitterly (Luke 22:59-62).

Failure often evokes tears. The universal experience of human shortcomings reminds us that we often fall short of our goals. Made in the image of God, we choose standards and purposes, and flinch when we fail to reach them. Each of us is aware that within us we have the capacity to reach the highest good, as well as the potential to do poorly. Sometimes we succeed and sometimes we fail.

Disciplined athletes competing for the Olympics remind us that sometimes even our best efforts fall short. The field of play and the workplace are replete with the tears of failure. Stung by the superior performance of someone else, we cry tears of disappointment for having come so close—and missed our mark.

Not that we always weep because we have performed poorly. Sometimes we hurt with a standard we (or someone else) set. We feel we did not measure up. We wrestle with the idea of having failed God or having failed in some sacred duty. Whether we believe we have failed God, our family, our friends, our country, or ourselves, we are burdened by our deficiencies and often judge ourselves harshly.

Perception of Failure and Self-Esteem

The pain of failure hurts deeply. Whenever we fear that we have failed in some way, it is helpful to check our perceptions for accuracy to verify if we have actually failed. Most of us rate ourselves so poorly that we often assume we have failed when we have not. If we ask ourselves to be specific about how we have failed at the onset of our tears, we can save ourselves unnecessary grief.

Unfortunately, whether we have actually failed or not matters little to most of us; if we feel we have failed, we hurt. Years of counseling depressed people has taught me that human beings measure success or failure subjectively. If we perceive that we have failed, we usually conclude that we have failed—regardless of evidence to the contrary.

Most of us move through the day with a steady stream of assignments we complete successfully. When we mishandle or fail to "succeed" at one task, we may interpret our entire day as "unsuccessful." Asked how we are doing, most of us reply that our day has been a disaster. We allow one event to color our assessment of the day because we give one negative experience more significance than the day's positive experiences.

Such interpretations almost always give us a distorted view of our day—and of ourselves. An accurate check of our day would reveal that we were successful at most things we attempted. But we have learned to dismiss our successes and focus on our mistakes. We spend time reviewing our failings, while discounting or ignoring our accomplishments.

Those of us who practice this selective "trashing" of ourselves should not be surprised to discover how little we value ourselves. Convinced that we have failed an entire day because of one difficulty, we reduce our self-esteem further by reliving only our mistakes. We spend little or no time acknowledging our successes.

Self-esteem is maintained or damaged by our capacity to acknowledge and affirm our positive experiences. Distorted reviews of our days naturally end in discouragement. Time spent mostly reviewing our failures can only lead to depression. If we also dismiss or ignore our successes, we accentuate our low estimate of ourselves and remain out of touch with our value as persons. To reject or devalue the good we accomplish is to foster low self-esteem.

Failing to reflect on our successes means treating ourselves inaccurately and unfairly. When we spend most of our time reviewing our faults, we develop self-hate and undermine self-worth. We aggravate the negative cycle of low self-esteem by dismissing positive experiences and thus confirming our sense of worthlessness. If we have already attuned to dissonance, we miss the resonant notes and find less and less in ourselves to like.

Some of us add to our low self-esteem by constant negative self-talk. We become depressed largely because we maintain ongoing destructive conversations with ourselves. Exaggerating our mistakes, we blow issues out of proportion. Reviewing negative incidents in our minds, we dismiss positive experiences.

Releasing the Captive: Breaking the Cycle of Irrational Thoughts

How can we escape this irrational and destructive emotional cycle? The first remedy is to quit "featuring our failures." We often shed tears of failure because we mislabel isolated events as "universal." We tell ourselves that "all we do is fail," that all we did today was "mess up," and that we can't "do anything right." In fairness to ourselves and our valuable contributions to the day, we need to challenge such lies. We are far more than any one experience and we need to be honest with ourselves about our successes. We can practice fairness by refusing to reduce our whole day to one event.

A helpful personal exercise is to increase our awareness of what we say to ourselves during the course of the day. By listening to our thoughts, we can check ourselves for accuracy, interrupt half-truths that have become lies ("I did nothing right today," "I am a failure," etc.), and refocus our thinking on the day's successes. Listening carefully to what we say to ourselves, we can keep our defeats in perspective. If we exaggerate the size of our failures, they falsely take on an importance they don't deserve. A careful check of our thoughts will give us a chance to learn how we trick ourselves with our self-talk. We can then see our mistakes for what they are and then control their power to overwhelm us.

Tears of failure suggest an opportunity for reflection. We need time to examine a situation calmly. A calm evaluation may reveal that what we thought was a failure is not actually so. Taking stock, we may discover what the true problem is.

Tears of failure may also offer us an opportunity to face reality. We may confirm that we have, in fact, failed in a particular way. A careful, balanced perspective gives us a more accurate understanding of our actions. Such inventory of our tears allows us to identify the nature and size of our failure—and more clearly point to any repair we may still make.

Embracing Our Failures

Tears of failure not only offer us a chance to determine whether we have failed or not, they also give us a chance to accept our mistakes and acknowledge defeat. Once we establish that we have failed, we have a chance to accept our fallibility by recognizing the reality of failure.

She sighed as she looked out the window of my office. Then she stood up and took full measure of what she was about to say: "It's hopeless, you know. . . . I've sat here telling myself that if I did this, or tried that, or succeeded in doing something else—that we (referring to herself and her husband) could make it. . . . But I've repeated this to myself and to you before. It's time to quit kidding myself. . . . It's over." She said the last few words with a finality I had not heard before, then added, "The best thing I can do right now is accept the fact that it's over." Looking down at the floor, she sighed again and said, "I guess it's really been over for quite a while now—I just didn't have the courage to say it. Maybe I didn't want it to be so. I feel so defeated . . . it's like I'm giving up." She began to cry again and said, "It's been dead for a while, and I just didn't want to admit it. But I know now. There's nothing I can do to make it work by myself."

Sometimes the process of accepting the inevitable is slow. The failure of marriages on which we have worked so long is hard to come to terms with. The loss of a job we've worked so hard to keep is difficult to face. The distance in a family tie we wanted so badly to hold close is painful.

The father of a non-responsive son shared his plight with me over dinner:

> I had to finally tell myself that I couldn't maintain the relationship all by myself. I was sick and tired of begging him to keep in touch with me. But it suddenly hit me that I couldn't control whether he called me, kept in touch . . . or even wanted to see me. I had to let go; it wasn't worth the pain of hoping and waiting and then being disappointed. He's on his own, and I'm going to let him decide when he wants to be in touch with me again. After all, he's thirty-two years old, and he's got to choose if he does or doesn't want a relationship with me. I give up—I can't make it work.

Sometimes the things we want most are not in our control. Sometimes the things we work for hardest are not in our reach. Abraham and Sarah failed to conceive a child for almost the length of their marriage. The priest, Eli, failed twice as a father before he "parented" Samuel as a prophet. Saul failed Israel as king; David failed his marriage; Elijah failed his faith. Peter failed to acknowledge his Master; Paul failed to follow Christ until Stephen's death.

The question is not whether we can avoid failure, but what we do once we have failed. Tears of failure are probably the first acknowledgment that we have missed our goal. To acknowledge defeat is to begin a process of separation from our loss that gradually enables us to move on to new challenges, hopes, and excitement about life. To reach this positive perspective, we must make sure we distinguish between accepting failure and succumbing to defeat.

Failure and Defeat

Failure is a normal occurrence for all human beings. None of us are perfect. It is natural to face many failures in life, but failures can teach us how to live more effectively.

There is a significant difference between failing and being defeated. To fail is to acknowledge that we have made mistakes. To feel defeated for a brief time is also normal as we come to terms with our weaknesses. But when feelings of defeat continue, we may decide give up to. The defeated spirit does not rise up to start again; the broken will within us may decide to try no more.

We fail to learn from our challenges only when we fail to rise from defeat—and move on. In a speech often delivered to his players, coach Vince Lombardi of the famed Green Bay Packers said: "The important thing is not whether you've been knocked down; it's whether you get up again, and get going."

No mistake or failure is serious enough to justify our permanent surrender. The apostle Peter, having failed Christ at least three times, struggled to understand that Christ had forgiven him and that quitting was unnecessary. We can all fail and start anew.

To feel permanently defeated is to believe that one failure in our lives is powerful enough to erase all future efforts. The disciple Judas apparently made that specific assumption for he took his own life after betraying Jesus Christ. Perhaps he concluded that there was absolutely nothing he could do to repair the damage. Judas could have been a wonderful model of Christ's grace in people's lives—but he didn't give himself the option.

If any one event in our life leads us to conclude that we are worthless, or gives us a sense of permanent defeat, we must immediately question our judgment. Is any one failed event worth our whole future? We must guard ourselves against such unfair and distorted evaluations. The first signal that we are adopting defeat as a permanent outlook on life could be continued periods of tears.

Other signs include a lack of interest in any project; continuous and paralyzing depression (more intense than usual); loss of appetite and sleep, or "binge" eating and excessive sleeping; behavior that our friends report as out of character for us; loss of interest in personal grooming and hygiene; difficulty in performing routines we are accustomed to (such as getting out of bed, dressing, and going to work in the morning); lack of concentration and forgetfulness, especially not keeping schedules or appointments; destructive thoughts that occur more than once, such as wanting to kill ourselves; uncharacteristic irritability or preoccupation; unusual mood swings; or irrational or dysfunctional reasoning.

Any combination of two or three of these signs of depression is reason to call a family doctor, a therapist, or a minister for help. Such traumatic times should not be spent in isolation from family or loved ones, nor should the individual make private decisions of any importance. Under such stress, judgment and perspective are impaired. If the warning signs are present, we should no longer make decisions by ourselves. Judas, for example, went away by himself to take his own life; he might have been a "recovered" disciple if he had kept in touch with the small community of believers—each of whom had also betrayed Christ. (Recall that in the Upper Room, where Christ declared one of the disciples would betray him, each asked if they were he—for each had considered it. When the mob arrived, all the disciples abandoned Christ.)

If self-defeat does not control us, however, we are in a safe position to journey through a process of recovery in the midst of any failure. Most people who travel through failures to healing and renewal negotiate three issues: acknowledgment, release, and re-engagement. This threefold movement takes failure seriously without allowing it to overwhelm us.

Acknowledgment

By accepting of our failings, we gain permission to acknowledge that we are fallible creatures. When we acknowledge failure we confess our finitude. We are not perfect; we cannot always succeed. To acknowledge that we have unsuccessfully completed a project, a hope, or a promise is to declare our awareness of a weakness or a mistake. We are taking responsibility for a failed event or behavior.

Taking such responsibility does not mean we are not declaring ourselves failures. It means that we are declaring a given goal, design, or action failed. Tears of failure alert us (and others) to the pain we feel at having to declare defeat. Identifying the reality that some of our goals are unreachable, or that we cannot change particular outcomes, is a realistic embracing of our limitations.

When plans we set forth fail, acknowledging defeat means ending our pursuit of those goals, or at least the ways we pursue them. Tears in such instances are actually a confirmation that letting go involves a loss dear to us. To fail at anything is painful; to shed tears is to acknowledge that importance.

Accepting our failure is an admission that we are not perfect. The reality of being imperfect helps us accept ourselves as we are: fallible human beings who do not need to pretend that we are otherwise.

Release

Shedding tears often signals that we are being released from the "captivity" of our failed goals. The physical, emotional, and spiritual discharge that tears offer us is a welcome unburdening. God gives us tears as a way of channeling the unspoken and unidentified pain we carry. Tears allow us to be delivered from the anguish of permanent disappointment.

Tears also wash away the heaviness of our loss; they prepare us for shouldering failure and reality. They strengthen our capacity to face the moment and the next day. The recurring ebb and flow of tears are like ocean waves gently washing away the footprints on the shore—the footprints of our failures. Our tears, then, are not rude interruptions in the healing of our lives; in fact, they are allies in the journey to cleansing and releasing. Sometimes we need to cry in order to "link up" with our next step of recovery and hope.

Tears, then, are physical stepping stones on the journey of renewal. The release and balance they provide us are essential to our personal survival and well-being. They bring us hope; they remind us that failure is not the last word.

Christ, writhing on the cross, cries out with the agony of a failed mission to call Israel to follow. Yet from the tears of Calvary, where disciples also share the pain of failure, Christ moves through the silence of a tomb to emerge on Sunday as the victor of a dream gone dead. We who follow share not only in the agony of the defeat, but in the birth of tomorrow's hope beyond the tears.

Reengagement

We who have failed gradually pass through a room of tears and walk into new daylight. Shedding the weight of failure takes time, but there are rewards. The gift of tears allows us a new freedom to believe again.

We must first begin to believe in ourselves again. Failure leaves us scarred; we who survive must overcome our suspicion that we are a failure and revive our damaged confidence. We must also shed the distortion of low self-esteem and renew our belief that we make positive contributions to life every day. We have the right to believe in ourselves as capable and valuable human beings because God has given all of us good gifts and adds grace to each of our failures. God asks us, then, to be faithful—both to the image of God inside us and to the hopes and purposes ahead of us (1 Corinthians 4).

The tears we shed in failure prepare us for the reality of life in an imperfect, fragile world. The gift of failure and survival constitutes the renewed hope that each time our efforts fail we can survive—and start over. Our tears of failure remind us of our constant need for grace and for God's constant willingness to grace us out of our defeats.

Tears of failure thus become our first sign of faith in the future. Failed hopes and goals give us a more realistic picture of the expectations we have placed upon ourselves. Now clearer and more appropriate hopes can be born; we can re-engage in dreaming with a better view of what we can promise and accomplish. Equipped with the humility of failed experiences and a new desire to conquer, we become dreamers and doers with a new vitality and a keen sense of confidence that "he who began a good work in you will carry it to completion on the day of Christ Jesus" (Philippians 1:6). We understand more than ever that we are not working alone. We are given new chances daily; we are graced when defeated. We see ourselves able to succeed far more than we will ever fail. The good news of Jesus Christ, as Paul discovered in his limitations, also gives us strength: "My grace is sufficient for you."

Chapter 4

Tears of Fatigue

The weary soul weeps tears that bathe its worn-out soil.

SOME OF US HAVE NEVER BEEN GIVEN permission to rest. If "idle hands are the devil's workshop," as the British adage asserts, then for many of us in this culture, busyness is next to godliness. We live in a society that worships overextension and perpetual activity. Other societies laugh at Americans for "working at leisure." Many of us struggle with finding permission to rest or slow down. Sometimes only the tears of fatigue remind us that we are exhausted.

I placed the letter on Charlotte's desk as I wheeled out the door and said, "If you can get that letter out this afternoon, that will be great!" I said, assuming she would answer with her usual positive reply. But as I was about to close the door, the irritation in her face slowed me down. "Well, I doubt it! Not that it matters, but it won't be anytime soon!" she replied. I mumbled, "Okay," as I was late for a church member's surgery; but I made a note in my mind to find out more about the intensity in her reply when I returned.

When I returned to the office, Charlotte was not at her desk, but down the hall in the printing room. She looked as if she had already been crying, and her eyes filled up with tears as I came in. "I wanted to follow up on our exchange as I ran out the door this morning, Charlotte," I said. "You seemed visibly upset, and I didn't have time to ask you much. Can you tell me how you're doing? Is this a good time to talk?"

She began crying harder as she shook her head to acknowledge my question, then said: "I'm upset! Everyone around here just hands me things to do on the run and never stops to ask me how much I already have—and whether I can get it done when they want it." Her voice grew stronger as her feeling grew deeper: "I'm sick and tired of being taken for granted around here! I'm not a machine! People come into that office all day long asking me to do this and that, telling me when and how much to do, just like they owned the place! I have 600 bosses, and all of them think I have nothing else to do but what they want done. . . . I'm sick of it!"

The anger in her voice was stifled at times by the tears, but it was clear that she was deeply disturbed and feeling overwhelmed. I reflected for a moment on how the church had been understaffed at for a while now and how all of us felt stretched to our limit. And though I had often told the staff to slow down when they needed to do so, Charlotte, among others, just kept overworking in order to compensate for the reduced staff.

Charlotte and I sat down and talked about her load of work, the constant pressure of deadlines, her sense of never getting finished, and the long hours she had been putting in at work. The more we talked, the more she cried. She was overdue for both rest and relief, and she needed someone to give her permission to stop. One of the things we discovered in the conversation was that as long as the rest of the staff kept working, Charlotte felt she needed to keep working. She was exhausted, but could find no moment when she felt free to catch up on her rest.

Charlotte is like many of us in regard to loyalty and work. She wants to do her part and has trouble asking for permission to slow down when tired. Caregivers in all walks of life struggle with the inability to take time out when they are overextended. Therapists, caregivers to others, have themselves wrestled enough with this need that counseling organizations have given it a name: Compassion fatigue. Ministers, nurses, physicians, social workers, therapists, and hospice volunteers all cross their physical and emotional limits. Few of us seem to know when we need to stop and rest. Charlotte's tears were a sign of her overextension.

Tears of fatigue are friendly reminders that our bodies need rest to recover and to work well. The biblical command for a sabbatical day was a clear set of "directions" given by the Creator to emphasize the crucial importance of rest for the care and optimum maintenance of our bodies. As Inventor of this miracle called the human body, God wanted us to appreciate its optimum purpose and performance. The divine Maker created us for excellence, and made us to be fueled by appropriate interruption and recovery.

The biblical warning to rest was at first a simple rule designed to be followed by a childlike people:

> Six days you shall labor and do all your work, but the seventh day is a Sabbath to the Lord your God. On it you shall not do any work, neither you, nor your son or daughter, nor your manservant or maidservant, nor your animals, nor the alien within your gates . . . (Exodus 20:9-10).

Sabbat in Hebrew means to cease, to desist; the Jewish people were ordered to totally quit work on the seventh day of the week.

In the Genesis record, the entire creation is placed on hold to rest and to reflect on the seventh day: the ground was to lie fallow, the animals were to rest, and human beings were to set firm limits on their activities. The early laws were expanded in the Torah (the Law of the first five books in the Bible), which spelled out details of Sabbath observance for all creation. People were to pause one day a week and reflect on the Creator, and to remember God's purposes for creating. Periodically, even the land was to be left unplanted for one year so that it could recover its essential nutrients and produce in a healthful way.

The people of God matured in their understanding of the Sabbath, but also tried to ignore or avoid the divine command. They, like us, developed many exceptions that gave people permission to labor on the Sabbath under certain emergencies. As they did, we have found ways to cheat on resting, and seem to suspect that inactivity is an enemy, or a luxury to be indulged in or seldom allowed.

One reason God gives us tears is to alert us to fatigue. Our body is so conditioned that it needs interruption to recover its vitality. A cramped muscle, for example, can be used again only if it is allowed to relax. Our body, mind, and spirit also need rest and recovery. Unless we schedule rest into our work schedule (as God did with a body designed to sleep eight out of each twenty four hours), we deplete our natural reserves and trigger signals of exhaustion.

What are some of our body's clearest indicators of fatigue? We have already said that tears are frequently a sign of exhaustion. Any of us who are not normally prone to crying under the regular pressures of the day may find ourselves surprised when what we consider a minor event triggers a tearful response. Accumulated fatigue drains us, and, when our reserve energy is low, we surprise ourselves with a show of tears.

Some of the common bodily symptoms of fatigue include less patience, difficulty concentrating, mood swings, depression, loss of appetite, panic attacks, and illogical reasoning. "Burn out" is now a common term in work circles, as we understand the similarities between a burned-out motor and physical exhaustion.

Several issues make identifying fatigue important: (1) We can be mislabeled as "too emotional" by people who do not understand how overextended we are. (2) We may need intervention if excessive work requirements are generating regular episodes of exhaustion for us—and perhaps others. (3) If we identify fatigue as a major ingredient in our tears, we can interrupt destructive work cycles and provide constructive alternatives that better manage our energy, productivity, and time.

Tears of fatigue need to be taken seriously. They are our first line of protection against abuse and paralysis. Because so many times we are unaware of the damage we cause ourselves by overexertion, we need an internal alarm system that will caution us to slow down and examine our daily load at early stages of fatigue. As we spend time learning about the dynamics of fatigue, we will identify three different dimensions to exhaustion: physical, emotional, and spiritual fatigue.

Physical Fatigue

Although the simplest to identify of the three areas of fatigue, physical exhaustion may not automatically be recognized. In agrarian and industrial eras, workers knew when they were physically tired. But gone are the days when most of us earned our pay by performing demanding physical activities. Today, the two main challenges to getting adequate rest appear to be that we do not recognize when we are exhausted, and we don't know how to rest. Because we are less aware of physical exertion in the workplace, it is harder for us to identify physical fatigue.

Modern living has introduced new ways to tire us and tax our physical well being. We experience subtle expenditures of energy everyday. The average nurse in a hospital setting, for example, walks seven miles per day. A homemaker with two preschool-aged children walks an average of twelve miles each day. The computer age has changed the nature of work-related injuries. Office workers know the meaning of "carpal tunnel syndrome," an inflammation in the nerves and tendons of the arms caused by prolonged strenuous activities with the hands and wrist.

We appear to be schooled to "make every moment count" and to prize action in the United States. Americans are more inclined than Europeans or Asians to prefer additional pay over extended vacation time. Our tendency to reward overextension inspired psychiatric consultant Wayne E. Oates several years ago to coin the word "workaholic" in his book *Confessions of a Workaholic*.

An additional reason for overextension in the work place appears to be the fear of job security; people agree to work longer hours to safeguard against being released or replaced. Whether such motivation is a major source of anxiety or not, the fact is that many people overwork themselves, expect to overwork, and become desensitized to their body's needs.

The greater challenge to rest, however, may be that we simply don't know how to relax. Accustomed to filling our hours with activities, we are busier than any generation before us. Students of human behavior have identified us as a society that needs to be busy at every turn, always entertained, always restless and doing. Perhaps we come to tears because we ache inside for rest and distance from our labor.

How do we learn to rest in a frenzied world? First of all, we need to believe in rest. In order to make time for rest, we need to believe in its legitimacy and benefit for us. Believers who struggle with rest may remember how often the Scriptures talk about Christ resting: ten major "retreat" schedules are mentioned, in addition to his daily sleep and Sabbath observance (he wouldn't have had any followers if ignored the laws of the Sabbath). Most students of the Bible will recall the story of the resting Messiah on a boat, trying to sleep after the exhausting work of talking with and healing hundreds of people (Matthew 8 and Luke 8).

The gospel of Mark records how the busy Messiah interspersed intense moments helping needy crowds with periods of rest and leisure for himself and his followers. Christ balanced a heavy work schedule with the refreshment of rest and relaxation. Because he is the model for all who aspire to a Christian lifestyle, such juggling of work, rest, recreation, and leisure can be our primary model when we are controlled by overwork.

The very content of the word "recreation" expresses the purpose of relaxation and renewal: we are to "re-create" within us the essential elements that renew our vigor and passion for work and life. The most fulfilling way to work hard is to rest adequately—to renew the desire and the capacity for work.

We will allow ourselves to stop and rest if we see purpose and validity in the interruption of work. We gain the ability to give ourselves permission to relax by believing in rest. This is a positive acquisition. We need to give ourselves permission to stop.

But we must genuinely believe in the value of rest, take it seriously, and schedule it into our daily routines.

Understanding the sacred function of rest helps us learn to seriously believe in it. Rest renews us by inviting us to pause and reflect on the meaning of life, on the Creator who cares for us, and on a creation designed for our good. Worship is a weekly invitation to return to our first purposes, to remember our Maker, and to renew our inner being by reflection and review. The biblical worshiper was asked to abandon the distractions of labor once a week in order to understand what life and labor were all about.

A second important issue in learning how to rest is the capacity to set boundaries. Boundaries are the limits we set on what we do. The amount of time we allot to various activities needs to have clear definition. How long are we to work? What schedules are we bound by? Are we setting limits for labor and spaces for leisure? Unless we set boundaries for our schedules, we will have no time for rest—or anything else.

Setting boundaries also means establishing controls over other people's requirements of us. The expectations or demands of family, employers, coworkers, and friends can impose excessive schedules on us. We can expend a great deal of effort trying to meet inappropriate demands of people we care about and exhaust ourselves in the process. Having boundaries means being able to distinguish between what other people want from us, and what we believe we can and should do. When we set no boundaries between ourselves and others, we allow ourselves to be run over by others, and exhaust ourselves trying to please them. Without boundaries, we rarely meet our own expectations, because we have no clear limitations on the demands others make of us.

How to Rest

We learn how to rest, first of all, by scheduling leisure and rest into our schedule. We often schedule everything but rest into our routine. We need to safeguard rest by declaring it important enough to allocate certain schedules for it daily, weekly, monthly, seasonally, and annually.

Those of us who work outside the home need to look at the "energy flow" of our day, and find two or three places where we can interrupt its intensity. If an agreement with employers is in order, a conversation with coworkers and managers can elicit a plan that is beneficial to all. Bosses and managers respond to such suggestions the moment they understand the extent to which self-care affects morale in the workplace. Productivity and efficiency are characteristics of cared-for employees.

Fatigue can also be stacked up and carried to the weekend, when we likely will "crash." If we invite family members into a "family council" in which each member learns how he or she can help the other find relaxation and protection from overexertion, we gain helpful allies. We must learn to ask for what we need for relief and in the way of nurturing. We also must find ways to reciprocate the support we receive.

If we are exhausted, weekend schedules should be carefully examined. We tend to schedule too much, and even work too hard at leisure. Families and individuals need to take a long look at the requirements of the weekend; we sometimes transform them into catch-all schedules that make us dread the end of the week rather than look forward to it.

We all need interruptions in our routines. An intentional look at the intensity of work and home should help us plan creative moments when we catch our breath and recover from the constant push and shove of work. Even mini-vacations can be invigorating. Setting aside a twenty-four-hour period can change the pattern of our routines and give us the rest we need. Two couples with preschool children, for example, formed an agreement. On certain weekends, they alternated childcare. One couple cared for all the children one day, and the other couple took the children the next day. This allowed the couples to take several mini-vacations during stressful times throughout the year.

Family vacations can be another source of increased stress, rather than the respite and renewal they were designed to be. In a time of pressured work schedules and high demands, we need to plan wise family vacations that require minimal energy for travel, sightseeing, and physical exertion. All of us have heard the joke about the family who could hardly wait to get back to work so they could rest.

We also need leisure and renewal for ourselves individually— time alone to recover emotionally and spiritually. The next two sections discuss the concepts of emotional and spiritual self-care.

Emotional Fatigue

We are a people with more emotional requirements than any other generation. Sociologists tell us that our ancestors 100 years ago met as many people in a lifetime as we meet today in one year. We also require more of ourselves; not only are more people working multiple jobs, but more people are single parents working full-time outside the home.

If physical fatigue is difficult to recognize at times, emotional fatigue is even harder to identify. The emotional requirements of occupations, family living, and everyday crises have an invisible but powerful effect on us. Many of us do not account for the energy expended by emotional experiences. Family caregivers who provide primary assistance to family members with Alzheimer's disease attest to the emotional drain that such care requires. We need recovery time from the drain of caregiving of all kinds.

Nurses, social workers, and therapists are particularly vulnerable to emotional exhaustion. Like any family caring for an invalid kin, such people face the strain of daily emotional requirements that sap energy. "Compassion fatigue" needs attention. How do we care for ourselves when we are emotionally drained?

We must first acknowledge that we can reach emotional limits just as we reach physical limitations. Recognizing our boundaries is the first step in acknowledging our need for rest.

Emotional fatigue requires interruption and relaxation. Those of us managing daily stress in the care of others must understand that we are better care providers when we take care of ourselves emotionally. Tears of fatigue should alert us to a need to stop.

My father developed Alzheimer's during the last two years of his life, and my mother was determined to care for him at home. My brothers and I initiated all the medical programs for which he was eligible in order to reduce our mother's load, including visiting nurses, hospital equipment, county assistance for personal hygiene, and regular visits by church members and friends. As she did not drive, we also helped our mother arrange trips for shopping, food, church, and social engagements. My youngest brother handled her finances to further reduce the stress.

Although her sense of humor and her willingness to talk about her hopes and fears helped reduce some of her stress, she needed to get away from the daily chores at home in order to care for my father without burning out. My brothers and I knew that if she didn't get away or take breaks, she would grow depressed, angry, or resentful. In order to give our mother breaks, my brothers and I made sure she left town for brief visits with family and friends. We also called her frequently. We understood that people who care for loved ones can feel guilty for resenting the constant requirements of caregiving; we also knew that it is the uninterrupted cycle of work that robs people of the joy of serving.

Tears of fatigue should also introduce us to the need for processing experiences that we live with daily. Church members dying of cancer have taught me that we regularly need to talk through our fatigue over endless days of sickness, treatments, procedures, and surgeries.

Emotional fatigue is a natural response to hours spent absorbing stress and tension. We need moments and places where we can leave "the madding crowd" to recover perspective. Jesus Christ had moments when he needed to get away from the pressure of the crowd. He even had specific places where he went in order to find solitude and peace. The garden of Gethsemane was probably a favorite quiet place, offered to him by a wealthy family that understood his need for privacy.

Christ frequently went to Bethany, to the home of Lazarus, Martha, and Mary, good friends who nurtured him and gave him "space." We also note that at times he left Jewish territory in order to find privacy in Gentile quarters (his trip to the Decapolis is an example). The Gospels remind us that "he withdrew into a quiet place" to rest on several occasions.

Sometimes we are so emotionally drained that we misread our own feelings. Married partners who are emotionally spent frequently come to me ready to leave their marriages. Under emotional duress, we often conclude that we are emotionally empty or that the feelings we do possess are all negative. We need emotional rest so that we may gain time and perspective to assess the source of our burnout.

Quite often our primary relationships have little to do with emotional burnout. We are victims of a steady accumulation of stress factors, coupled by our tendency to discount or ignore our own unmet needs and unreplenished resources. Our dismay with primary relationships is that we often expect our loved ones to guess that we are depleted and provide us with unrealistic measures of nurture.

A close examination of emotional emptiness will usually reveal that we have expended significant amounts of personal energy in a variety of places without refueling emotionally. To survive in a demanding and often impersonal world, all of us need places where our resources are replenished.

We need to be intentional about replenishing spent emotional energy. Our failure to take our needs seriously will leave us depleted. In order to survive the constant output of our emotional energy we need to follow at least two suggestions: (1) We need to be intentional about replenishing our emotional energy, willing to seek out people who energize us, and plan quality time with them as a necessity. (2) We need to learn to ask for emotional support, emotional space, and emotional care when we need it. Even those who love us most cannot guess what our needs are; the more clearly we can ask for what we need, the better our loved ones can respond.

Such self-care means that at times we need to ask for psychic space in order to catch up with ourselves. Jesus Christ was very intentional about such needs: "Sit here, while I go yonder and pray. . . . Remain here, and stay awake," he told his disciples. The Master claimed time and space for himself to process the intense emotional content of his ministry with people. Immersed in the pain and struggle of human affairs, Jesus needed time to discern how best to participate in other people's lives.

Spafford Ackerly, a psychiatrist in Louisville, Kentucky, described a psychological moratorium as an emotional time-out that many of us need in our personal journey so that we can catch up with ourselves emotionally. Significantly, most of us have difficulty giving ourselves permission to take time out from vocational or employment pursuits. Our society tends to label such interruptions as an irresponsible waste of time.

My father studied to become a concert pianist for years. He once told me of a conversation he had with pianist Arthur Rubinstein, in which my father shared his frustration with bouts of emotional void. Rubinstein replied by declaring that there were periods in his own life when he was so emotionally spent that he could not practice or perform adequately. He eventually learned to give himself permission to retreat and recover emotionally. All of us need such retreats at junctures in our life.

The value of interruption and retreat is that it provides us fuel for recovery. Distance and calm are unique features that gift us with perception. Armed by the renewal that change and interruption provide, we breathe new air and see things in new ways. The "tightness of thinking" that controls our emotions relaxes. We recover peace and gain hope. We begin again to believe that joy is possible, that we can sort through the "parliament of shouting demands" and regain focus for our life.

> Weeping may remain for a night, but rejoicing comes in the morning (Psalm 30:5).

Spiritual Fatigue

Most believers appear little acquainted with the seasons of the soul. Many people seem to believe that a spiritual journey is a steady positive climb toward excellence and intimacy with God. The biblical witness of many tearful pilgrims seems often overlooked. Our tears of fatigue may be tears of spiritual depletion.

It can be difficult to determine when we become spiritually depleted. At various times in our spiritual development we cross spiritual plateaus in which growth is interrupted. Such times are characterized by a lack of enthusiasm or interest in religious activities, an emotional withdrawal from community, a detached numbness, lethargy, and low-grade depression (fifth-century monks called this state "acedia").

Several of our biblical heroes experienced spiritual fatigue. Moses, tending Jethro's flock in the desert, wanted little more than privacy and distance when he was disturbed by the God of the burning bush. He argues with God hoping to retain his isolation. Saul, struggling with depression and a selfish disposition, cries and feels abandoned by God. Elijah, fleeing Jezebel, withdraws into a cave and seeks isolation—not too long after a stunning display of courage and faith before the prophets of Baal. Peter, wounded by his own betrayal of the Messiah, struggles to hold on. Paul, stunned and blinded on a Damascus road, withdraws to Arabia to rethink his entire belief system.

There are certain things we need to do when we are spiritually depleted. First of all, we need to recognize our condition so that we do not demand too much of ourselves. Times of spiritual depletion are not occasions for new projects or creating deadlines for spiritual vitality. We need to acknowledge that our spiritual cupboard is empty and give ourselves time to replenish our depleted spiritual resources.

We can begin by declaring ourselves in need of rest and by withdrawing from the demands of service and leadership. Emotional and spiritual distance go hand in hand; we must find ways to divest ourselves of excessive requirements. We need time out spiritually, and the best way to get it is to explain our need and ask for a recess from overpowering responsibilities. Paul was probably blinded at Damascus for at least two reasons: (1) symbolically he became a walking model of spiritual blindness for all to recognize; and (2) the loss of sight also rendered him dependent, depriving him of any notions of religious leadership or service for a time. Literally speaking, he was to be led around for a while and served.

All of us need to accept periods of rest. These moments give us rich opportunity for reflection, a powerful gift we can rarely exercise when busy. There is a parallel in music. Music is enriched by pauses. While there is no music in a rest, there is the making of music in it. In a like manner, people experiencing spiritual fatigue are spiritually enriched by carefully placed pauses in their lives.

There may be frequent tears in our journey through a spiritual wasteland. But we can gain courage from our biblical companions. After all, Moses waited in the desert and wondered if he has lost sight of his first faith; and Paul was lonely and isolated, suspected both by old friends and the Christian community he embraced. Both of these pilgrims gave up tired portions of their old faith long before they fully grasped visions of their new faith.

When we face a spiritual wilderness, we must recognize the need for dependence on community. It is a believing community that prays for us and understands the importance of our need for "spiritual detours." Congregations can encourage us as we struggle on the periphery of faith. They can also take initiative in providing us sabbaticals and holidays when we need space from our assignments. Ministers and lay people alike should be able to request relief from certain responsibilities they have shouldered for a while. Such models of human stewardship can then become far better examples of Christian maturity than the recurring image we have in our congregations of the overextended, success-ridden minister or layperson.

Spiritual fatigue asks each of us to take God's temple (our bodies) seriously, and to seek to make our bodies responsible instruments of God's will. The worn-out follower needs care in order to provide care to others. Military organizations have met this human need by scheduling rest and recovery breaks for people consistently under stressful work conditions.

Our rested and renewed soul can soar again. A mind at peace can imagine new dimensions of belief. Our strengthened limbs can serve again. Tears of fatigue open detours to new space we hadn't seen before; they bless us with permission to rest from labor and to recover from exhaustion. Such retreats return us refreshed and stronger than when we left the path.

The early church celebrated Christ's resurrection by worshipping on the first day of the week. As believers, our interruption of routine on the first day of the week is intentionally designed to begin with worship, so that we regain purpose and perspective as we reflect on the nature of God, on our own life, and on our future. Worship calls us to stop, to look back, to absorb the present, and to look into the future—all in the context of a divine purpose.

We are not the same for having left the fray; we are stronger for having "laid down by the still waters." In this tiring world, we are more compassionate for shedding tears of fatigue and recovering our strength.

Chapter 5

—◆—

Tears of Fear

My tears, I fear, express the dread that lives inside.
So I must cry until the scare is gone.
My tears will leave; but will the fear? Be gone!

I HAD BEEN HER PASTOR FOR THREE YEARS. She called to make an appointment, but said nothing about her reason for coming to see me. Married and the mother of two children, she was part of a model family in our community. But the moment she walked into my office, her troubled face signaled the pain she carried. At first she spoke evenly and quietly; she had decided to share something with me, but she was afraid to talk about it.

Then, as her eyes filled with tears, she described the physical abuse in her marriage. Her husband, who seemed to be a mild-mannered man, experienced bouts of temper that made him volatile and violent. She had managed to deal with the violence mainly by not provoking him. But now with children in the home, she was afraid for their welfare. As she spoke, she looked more frightened than sad. At times, her tears were interrupted by moments where she seemed to stiffen and brace herself.

I asked her the usual questions I had learned to ask about abusive situations: Had she spoken to anyone else about this behavior? Had she ever reported her husband's actions to local authorities? How aware was he of his problem? Had he ever sought help? Had she ever left him to protect herself? Had he, in fact, ever physically abused the children, as far as she knew? Between tears, she said that I was the first person she had mentioned the situation to. She went on to say that twice before, when she asked him to get help and threatened to speak to a third party, he had quit his job and forced the family to move to another town.

I asked if there was any possibility that he would talk with me or with someone else. She looked frightened again, and said he would go to no one. Abusive spouses often threaten more abuse if their partners press them to get help. I knew this because I was on the Family Abuse Center Board of our local shelter for battered spouses; moreover, our church secretary had been killed by her husband just two years before this meeting. Spouses and families can be paralyzed by the suggestion that the abuser be confronted as this makes the victims vulnerable to more harm. She went on to say that he had told her many times that he would lose his job if either one of them ever talked to someone outside the family about their "private life." Many of us come to the clergy first when we are frightened. During these times, we need support to manage our pain and we hope to preserve our privacy.

Physical abuse is just one of many behaviors in our country that provokes hidden fear. Tears of fear are shed every day because of other experiences. The bullied student crouches in a corner of the playground, choking back the tears that fall on his brown lunch bag, emptied by the hands of a stronger classmate. The hungry mother of three, unemployed and waiting in the food line, weeps as she watches her children trust her with tomorrow, while she fears tomorrow herself. The young wife listens for a report of casualties in a war fought thousands of miles away, and holds back her tears as she catches her throat at the naming of each soldier killed in action. The widow in a modest retirement center reads an eviction notice from the health authorities, and wonders where she will go and how she will survive. The helpless father sheds an anxious tear anticipating a phone call that may bring news his severely depressed son has taken his own life. Far from home, the college student faces the first day of school on a busy, impersonal campus, and buries his head in his pillow to muffle his sobs.

We all have cried tears of fear. As children, the unknown dark beneath our beds was perhaps our first dreaded cause for tears. When we thought we were lost from our parents, we felt terrified and our eyes welled up with tears. Some of us have been scared to tears by illness or death. Some of us even remember crying over a failed test.

As adults we have learned to disguise our fears and pretend we are neither anxious nor alarmed. Because we mask our grownup fears, we frequently cry tears of fear without understanding the emotions behind them. The symbolic language of tears expresses what we often cannot bring ourselves to say—that we are frightened.

What makes fear so difficult an emotion to talk about? Do we suspect that to acknowledge fear is to increase its power over us ? Do we strive so much to keep control over all our "awkward" emotions that to dwell on fear might make us lose control over our deepest apprehensions? Whatever our motives, it appears that we are so afraid of fear that we have disguised it even from ourselves—and struggle to recognize it. Perhaps a first step toward our management of fear as adults is to recognize its presence in us, and acknowledge that fear may be as powerful an emotion as anger.

What we assert in these pages is that fear is a significant human force, and that we need to respect and identify its influence over us. We also affirm that fear need not become our enemy, and that our tears of fear can help us identify and confront those destructive feelings which hold us captive to anxiety and dread. How can we do that?

*   *   *   *   *

Tom, a quiet, polite, affable college junior, had talked with me several times, but this was the first time he had called me with a trembling voice. "Do you have a few minutes?" he asked. "Could I meet you at the church as soon as possible? I hate to bother you at home like this, but I'm kind of worried about something—and I guess I just need to talk about it. . . . I'm kinda scared." I quickly said yes, knowing that Tom wouldn't call me unless he was really hurting.

When I arrived at the church, he was waiting for me, wearing a troubled face. As soon as we got in the office, he covered his face with his hands, and then uncovered moistened eyes. As he began to talk, tears fell. He explained that he was overcome with a panic inside that was paralyzing him. Although he was an excellent student, he had tried to study for the past four days but his mind would "lock up." He would stare for hours at information but he could not retain it. Several times he had broken out in a cold sweat. When he tried to sleep he couldn't. His mind would race and his breathing would get shorter and shorter, until he wound up hyperventilating. Tom said he was scared to death.

Tom had no prior history of physical or emotional problems. Shy and unassuming, he had driven himself to study harder than he ever had before. At the same time he found a need for community that he had rarely felt before. Caught between the pressure to survive in college and the need for interpersonal contact, Tom was suddenly fearful that he would no longer be able to maintain the required study pressure to stay in school. He wasn't sure what he wanted to do with his life. He found himself unmotivated, and he was frightened by his inability to control his fears.

Fear is a natural reaction we have to losing control. We lose control, or never have control, over many events each day. While we know we cannot control all that happens to us, most of us enjoy a capacity to control our own actions and reactions. Discovering that certain actions and behaviors are not under our control can cause us serious fright. Such fears are called "panic." We may become especially panicked when we feel that we are losing control over our own thoughts.

The Anatomy of Fear

When we are afraid, we react physiologically to the notion of fear. Our brain sends orders to our glands to release adrenaline into the blood system; our sweat glands activate. Adrenaline immediately increases the heart rate and respiration accelerates. The blood supply rushing through the veins places the entire body on "full alert." The brain stem (the lower part of the brain) sends survival messages to the part of the brain that controls emotions. We may begin physical movements to protect or defend ourselves. The cerebral cortex, the creative, evaluative, reasoning part of our brain, may or may not be engaged in this response as it is a voluntary system, activated only by our conscious decision to respond.

All of us have at some time experienced fear and dread. Our anxieties have brought tears to our eyes. Sometimes tears of fear are brought on by extreme circumstances. The pregnant thirty-three year-old mother of two who suddenly learns that she has breast cancer is caught off guard and cries tears of fear. The abused child cries tears of terror at the return of an abusive parent. The anxious mother, waiting in the doctor's office for a report on vital signs of life within her quiet womb, struggles to contain the tears that channel all her fears. The stunned businessman—left alone after being informed that his services are no longer needed by a company for which he has worked more than thirty years—cradles the tears that fall in his idle hands. The terrified father—forced to identify his oldest son, a victim of a fatal accident—clears his throat and allows himself to cry.

We may run away from important opportunities because of our fears. We may become paralyzed by our fears or we may overreact to our fears. But we can also discover places where some of our anxious tears are our friends. Weeping gives our fears a voice. Our task, then, is not to discourage tears of fear, but to identify their presence, understand their meaning, and reduce the negative power some fears hold over us.

Three Options

When we feel vulnerable and unprotected, we become afraid. Fear is a natural response to the possibility of danger, injury, loss, or trouble. Safety and security are important to small infants; those needs continue to be significant to us at every age. The vulnerable child may run, cry, or scream when afraid. What does a vulnerable adult do? Most of us have been socialized (trained) by our community to respond in "more mature" ways. According to trauma experts, we tend to react in one of three ways: flight (we try to escape); freeze (we become paralyzed by our fear); or fight (we defend ourselves vigorously).

The first evidence of fear may surprise and confuse us. Sometimes we run when we are afraid. Family members who can be physically overpowered have learned that escape is the best defense against some forms of abuse—where flight is possible. Abuse victims, unfortunately, will submit to repeated physical and emotional attacks, and will frequently seek refuge only if a child's safety is at issue.

The battered person has experienced physical abuse often enough to recognize some of the behaviors that precede offensive actions. Abusive people are creatures of habit, and victims soon learn to watch and listen for the clues that abusers give us: the louder voice, the more impatient tone, those first aggressive physical gestures, the forceful manner, the loss of control—all are signs that intimidation and abuse are around the corner. Escaping the immediate danger is the wisest thing a victim can do.

When frightened or attacked, some adults "freeze" rather than protect themselves. Traumatized people can be so intimidated emotionally that they become virtually paralyzed. We may surrender our rights under the pressure of an overpowering force. Paralyzed by our own fear of injury, or by the possibility of harm to a loved one, we commonly give in to the oppressive behaviors of a controlling partner. Freezing is not so much a chosen response to fear as it is a helpless capitulation under pressure. We often have no idea what to do when we are afraid. As the saying goes, we may be "frozen stiff" by fear.

Some people react to fear by fighting back. Disturbed by our anxiety, we may lash out at whatever appears to be scaring us. Although fighting back under fear sometimes gains us time and space by protecting us, we also are reacting immediately to a situation—and with intensity. Immediate and intense responses are rarely our best responses under pressure.

Managing Our Fears

Fear is a reaction to a perceived threat. How we interpret events has a lot to do with whether or not we feel fear. Much of our fear is learned. The child playing with a spider will not fear the spider until it stings her—or a parent scares her by reacting with fear themselves. As children, darkness was not scary unless it separated us from security and safety. Experience and information give us cause to fear. When we burn a hand, we learn to respect—or fear—fire. When injured, we learn to be afraid of those with whom we associate being hurt.

We have good reason to fear certain things: some actions and behaviors are dangerous and can injure us; and some situations are very unpleasant and possibly remind us of earlier experiences in which we were troubled or injured. Tears of fear are mainly shed because we remember or anticipate. We remember pain, discomfort, and danger. If we anticipate pain, discomfort, or danger again, we become anxious and fearful.

When we know specifically what scares us, we call it fear. When we feel afraid and cannot name the source of our distress, we usually call it anxiety. When we are struggling with fears, we usually can name them, given opportunity and perspective. If asked what it is that troubles us, we respond by identifying a potential or actual danger: We fear leaving the house at night in a troubled neighborhood because we are afraid we might be assaulted. We fear losing an important relationship, and we cry as we anticipate the loss. We fear trying new things, such as new jobs, because we are afraid we will fail.

Each of our responses to fear provides us with both risk and promise. When we flee in fear (flight), we may prevent some good opportunities from growing or we may avoid serious danger. When we freeze out of fear, we may become unable to engage in worthwhile activities or we may buy ourselves time by not jumping into difficult experiences prematurely. When fear causes us to fight we may overreact to situations or we may be mustering strength for an issue important enough to champion. How can we make fear, and the tears that fear produces, an ally and not an enemy? The following insights may be beneficial:

When fear prompts us to flee, we may use our "exit" as an opportunity to examine our situation from a safe vantage point. Fleeing can be helpful, if it gives us time to look at what has caused our fear. As children, some of our fears were imagined; as adults, stepping away from our fears may give us opportunity to determine which fears are real and which fears are imagined.

Those of us who work in churches have learned to pay attention to the early signals of fear that children give us. Children who flinch, draw back, or cry when we gesture with our hands may be reacting to fear from abuse by an adult. Some children hide from parents to escape abusive treatment; some teenagers get jobs or find other ways to stay away from home because of fear of maltreatment. We have good reasons to find ways to run from harm, and we may have to try different ways to flee at different ages.

Tears of fear may also prompt us to look at ways we may be running from fearful, but promising, opportunities. A young lady sat in my office and cried as she spoke of loving her fiancé—and announced that she was breaking her engagement and going home. She had been engaged twice before, once to this same man, but the engagements never led to marriage. Each time we had talked about her broken plans, she restated how much she wanted to marry and have children, and how much she loved her boyfriend. But each time the relationship entered a new level of commitment, her fears intensified.

We talked about her fears of betrayal in marriage, and eventually she identified the lack of trust she had in all men—because she had never trusted her father. She struggled for several years with her deep hopes of having her own family and with the fears that caused her to run every time the opportunity neared.

Fears can cause us to run from our deepest longings, and our tears may help us identify places where we need to pause and meet the cause of our fears. Fleeing from the pressure of the moment may be a good option, as long as our fears don't deny us the opportunity for very appropriate plans. The child who desperately wants to make the team, but cries because she's afraid she may not perform well, may need to challenge herself to overcome her fears because her skills are worth the risk. As a result, she may be rewarded with the deep satisfaction of making the team. The young man who flees every promotion because of the responsibility may need to back away and look at his options. He may find that momentary flight allows him to embrace the challenge as an opportunity for development and greater confidence.

When fear causes us to freeze, we have another opportunity to catch our breath, gain perspective, and prepare our response. Freezing, as a temporary reaction to fear, buys us time to size up our fears. Sometimes we blow our fears out of proportion. We need time for careful reflection to mentally trim our fears down to size.

Those who help us gain perspective under stress remind us that the mind's eye often sees fears as larger than they really are. We can use the paralysis caused by our fear as a time out from pressure to measure its size. The act of simply understanding the true nature of a fear has a way of shrinking it down to a manageable size.

Victor Frankl, the skilled Austrian psychiatrist who was a prisoner of war during the1940s, introduced the idea of "paradoxical intention" in the treatment of people paralyzed by fear. By suggesting to his patients that they try doing exactly what they feared (just as he had done), he succeeded in inspiring many people to tame their fears by "walking through them."

The stutterer was asked to stutter as much as he could—and found himself unable to stutter. The person afraid of the dark was encouraged to sit in the dark for a while—and discovered that the dark held no special power over her.

When our fears overpower us and control us, we may need a friend or a counselor to help us find freedom from their control. If our tears and our fears continue over long periods of time, we can feel helpless and permanently disabled. Telling a friend about our struggle with fear can be an empowering action. We may then find an ally who will listen to us and help us keep perspective.

When fears prompt us to fight, we may discover a hidden strength within us. The fighting spirit inside of us may be just what we need to overcome our fear. People known for their capacity to take risks report that courage is not the absence of fear, but a determination to overcome fear because they feel passionate about something. We all have this capacity.

Fearful tears can prompt us to look within ourselves again, to find not only what we fear, but what we are willing to fight for. William Wallace, the courageous Scottish hero celebrated for his passionate fight against English oppression, rallied his outnumbered, fearful peasant army into fighting for freedom by reminding them that their other option was to surrender—and to live with fear as a constant companion.

Wisdom and Fear

We need validation of our fears; we also need to learn when to flee, when to freeze, and when to fight. In some cases we may be so vulnerable that we need to find immediate protection from harm. Those of us who face physical and sexual abuse may need to take immediate action to guarantee safety.

We need to learn when to leave abusive relationships. Living in constant fear is both unnecessary and harmful. The turmoil and anxiety of abusive family ties can be traded for peace of mind and safety at temporary shelters, extended family care, or confidential places where we may go for protection.

Some losses generate the overpowering fear that we cannot survive without certain family members. We may be tempted to surrender to abusive and oppressive behaviors because we believe we must. To live without fear for our safety, we need to learn to set boundaries for family members who will not set boundaries for themselves. If some people will not discontinue destructive behaviors around us, we need to get away from them—and their power over us. We may need the intervention of police and other authorities to protect ourselves—but we can draw limits on behaviors we will not tolerate.

When we need financial help to gain freedom from destructive relationships, we can take initiative with abuse centers, churches, United Way agencies, child protective services, legal aid services, and other organizations. If we are held captive to abusive relationships by our fears about financial survival or personal safety, we need to ask for help. Otherwise we may choose a lifetime of fear; that is, living permanently with people who hurt and misuse us.

We who fear that we cannot function without a spouse that abuses us need to remember that we survived before we married them. Grief is normal when we find it necessary to distance ourselves from a loved one; but over time, we heal from our losses. Living in an abusive relationship means a perpetual period of fear and grief. Survivors of painful separations remind us that the human spirit is both resourceful and resilient; we can overcome our fears by concentrating on our capacities. Joining a group of "survivors" is one helpful plan for overcoming such fears. There are many such groups. They often meet in family abuse shelters, YMCAs, and crises centers.

Taking Charge

Sometimes we need courage to make decisions we have rehearsed many times in our mind. The encouragement of a friend, the steady support of a family member, or the nurturing care of a church care group may give us the extra support to declare an end to living under fear. Weary of shedding tears and of flinching in fear, we can declare our independence from such slavery and start a journey toward freedom.

Challenging our fears takes patience; no journey from fear is reached immediately. We need to celebrate cautious, small, first steps. New territory is conquered slowly. Our fears may still persist. But we needn't get discouraged when our progress is slow; some of us have spent years captured by our fears. We need to give ourselves permission to experiment with the courage and the new fears we feel as we try steps toward freedom.

We may choose several allies in this journey toward independence. Tears are our first helpers. As "carriers" of our feelings, they pour out our anxieties as we deal with internal dread. Whether they buy us time to muster strength, or divest us of the tension we feel as we prepare to tackle our troubles, tears are a healthy outlet for reducing our distress and for carrying away our initial fright.

Safe friends also help in our departure from fear. We may be so accustomed to being with abusive persons that we believe we have no choice in our companionships—but we do. We can choose to be with healthy and loving people who will support us in our flight to independence. We need to surround ourselves with people who encourage us, as opposed to people who feed our fears and discourage us. We need people who will not misuse us.

Church groups and other support groups may be the best place to find safe, secure, and healthy opportunities where we can rehearse our courage and plan our movement from fear. If such a caregiving group is not immediately available, we can speak to a minister or center director for information on starting such a group.

Our fears sometimes bring us to our knees. Christ in Gethsemane shed heavy tears of dread. He struggled with his tears for hours into the night. At dawn he found a new peace, a new courage, and a willingness to walk into the fear. Sometimes, we too need to travel through struggle and fear to find our courage. As did Christ, we find a strength we had not felt before. With that strength, we can find determination that carries us through agony to freedom from fear. Our new strength is the resurrection of our hope, our understanding that we may live without fear.

Not Alone

When facing the unpleasant and the scary, our greatest anxiety may be a feeling that we are all alone. We who believe in God know peace because we believe God's promise to "walk through the valley of the shadow of death" with us. With the psalmist who felt as vulnerable as a lamb in the wilderness, we hope for a faithful and strong shepherd who will walk beside us as we travel through our fear. That is God's assurance, too, as evidenced in his only Son. On the eve of his own death, this same God-with-us (Emmanuel) promised scared disciples that he would not leave them comfortless. He sent a presence, a holy comforter (to guide the disciples), and us through the treachery and dismay of human events.

The birth of Christ is our sure reminder that God has not left us to ourselves. The incarnation is our guarantee that God will not forsake us in our deepest trouble, but will walk beside us to the other side of fear, beside still waters, where we rediscover the peace that passes understanding.

Faith is not just a story in a book, but a reality that accompanies us to solid ground. Holy ground is merely ordinary dirt along the path where we look back and know that we've encountered the companion, God. Like Jacob, we too can then say, "Surely the Lord was in this place, and I knew it not."

Chapter 6

---•---

Tears of Frustration

I cry because I can do nothing else.
My hands are tied; my tears go free.

I HAVE WITNESSED MANY PEOPLE'S TEARS OF FRUSTRATION in my work. Our greatest hopes and dreams are sometimes dashed to pieces; we watch helplessly as things we've worked on for a long time fall apart. The causes of—or solutions for—these problems may be out of our control. The bitter tears that flow as a result are often a sign of defeat. Few experiences are more paralyzing than frustration over things that are out of our control.

He clenched his fist and buried it in his other hand as he spoke to me. He had just described repeated attempts at trying to forget that his wife loved another man; he grimaced as the taunting memory engulfed him. His eyes filled with tears, and his face flushed with anguish.

"Dan, I've tried every way I know to kill this doubt and fear inside my head. If I could just unscrew my brain, maybe I could stop the thoughts that won't go away. . . . I start wondering what it would be like to get my hands on him," he continued, beginning to cry again. "But I know that wouldn't help. So I think about her, and I wonder if I could somehow just reach into her mind and heart and yank every feeling for him right out. But I can't, and it drives me crazy. . . . I don't know what to do. But I know I can't go on like this!"

A woman in her forties came by to share her pain at being passed over several times in job interviews. Skilled and competent, she had applied several times to positions for which she felt qualified—only to be told that she was either on a waiting list or that someone else had been chosen for the job. Her frustration was evident in her drawn face. She felt a deep sense of injustice over being rejected before she'd been evaluated. She started crying as she recounted several times she felt discriminated against because of her gender or age.

The mother of a teenager sat at the table with me over lunch and expressed her anxiety over her daughter's behavior and her own inability to control it. Chewing her food intensely, she began to cry as she confessed her helplessness. As the single parent of three children, she felt that work, parenting, and financial pressures had reduced her life to a joyless and defeating routine. Ignoring her food, she swallowed hard and squeezed her frustration out in tears of hopelessness: "I don't know what to do. . . . I've tried everything I know. It simply hasn't worked. I'm not sure I'm fit to be my daughter's mother."

I barely recognized the college student's voice through her muffled tears. But she was also clearly disturbed. In broken sentences, I learned that her longtime boyfriend had left her—again. She voiced her frustrations about him. She unveiled the bitterness of investing herself deeply in a relationship that seemed to have no future. In solemn, hopeless tones, she described her helplessness.

All of these difficult instances illustrate the stirring agony of tears born from deep frustration. All of us have shed tears of frustration. We have faced the paralysis of coming to the end of our choices. We have encountered walls we could not break down. We have met situations over which we had no control. We have reached the limits of our endurance and have known what it means to stand by powerlessly as experiences we have not chosen take charge.

Sometimes there is no language to express how we feel when our hopes are defeated. Tears are often the only way we have to process extremely difficult and frustrating moments. Tears give us a tangible way to express our strongest emotions, and they allow us to expel frustration over matters beyond our control. Frustration comes because we care; its expression is one way our bodies connect pain and helplessness.

We must understand and appreciate tears of frustration in order to manage them. By doing this, we honor their value and interpret their meaning. We don't cry for no reason at all; we cry for specific reasons. Our capacity to identify and understand those reasons will help us process our feelings and our tears.

Understanding Frustration

Frustration is an inability to achieve chosen goals or hopes. The denial of specific aspirations or plans robs us of gratification. Frustration is a response that includes our thoughts, feelings, intentions, and spirits.

As people made in the image of God, we are all capable of dreaming, setting goals, setting expectations, and imagining possibilities. Our capacity to dream and to imagine are gifts from God. Because we are made to become creators ourselves, we nurture and develop our hopes, as well as expend significant time and energy pursuing our goals and dreams. We learn to value our thoughts and dreams as extensions of ourselves.

We feel stymied or denied when we cannot release our creative energies. When such energies are contained within us and hopes are denied, we respond with distress and dismay. The extent of our distress depends on the importance we ascribe to our expectations or dreams. Hopes or plans that shape our identities are especially important to us. Facing the possibility of losing highly valued dreams can be both painful and disturbing. Our perception that the ongoing pursuit of such goals is useless or impossible adds to the dynamic of helplessness and hopelessness.

Frustration is a natural reaction to the denial of an important hope. The possibility that we may never have what we aspire to, and have worked for, is very troublesome. When we become frustrated by events or changes not in our control, we feel helpless and inadequate. We also feel cheated.

Tears of frustration offer us a first clue that we are struggling with an issue that is very important to us. We struggle when we care.

Accepting Our Limitations

Frustration with unachievable hopes forces us to face our limitations. We cannot have all that we desire. We cannot control everything. And though we may work very hard to accomplish our ends, we sometimes will not get what we most want. Tears of frustration remind us that we are being denied something we care about—that we may have no other recourse but to accept what we cannot change.

As we come to terms with the value we place on particular goals and face the possible reality that our goals are unattainable, tears serve as rites of passage. Tears and frustration may signal our first recognition that a specific expectation has become important to us. And if we trust anyone else with our tears, those friends become witnesses to the value we've placed on certain unfulfilled hopes.

Tears may also help us see that we may not get what we desire. Those of us who have nurtured dreams for years can appreciate the full impact of realizing for the first time that it may not be attained. Tears of frustration may offer us the first measure of reality that permits us to acknowledge, even reluctantly, that a dream is unattainable. Tears can cleanse our insight so that our vision is no longer blurred by insistence on unrealistic hope or denial. When we face frustrated hopes, important questions emerge.

Are Prayers Always Answered?

If we are religious persons with deep convictions about God's presence in our life, we may have a perplexing set of questions with which to contend, such as: Is our failure to reach certain dreams evidence of our lack of faith or lack of persistence in asking? Is it our lack of faith that prompts us to quit hoping for certain things? Is our frustration also a disguised feeling of anger at God for not granting us what we sincerely asked for? The Judaeo-Christian believer brings to frustration a series of significant questions that challenge faith and our view of life.

The translators of St. Matthew's petitionary prayer in which Christ tells us to "ask, seek, and knock" remind us that he uses the present-progressive verb form. In English, this translates most accurately as "keep on asking, keep on seeking, keep on knocking," etc. This verb form obviously enjoins us to pray regularly and faithfully about matters important to us. What is still unclear to us, however, may be knowing how much asking is enough. In such a translation, we can be further haunted by the suggestion that we need to be more persistent than we have been previously.

Biblical evidence shows us that God did not grant his followers' every request. Moses, for example, did not enter the Promised Land; David could not build the temple he so desperately wanted to build; Jesus could not escape Golgotha; and Paul was not relieved of his "thorn in the flesh." Clearly, our best examples of faithful people in the Bible indicate that neither faith nor faithfulness determine "answered prayers." Sometimes our most fervent requests are not granted, and God does not always clearly explain why. But we do know that the God, who in Genesis pronounced creatures and creation free, must limit his divine intervention to preserve that freedom for us. If God always granted us everything we wanted (or everything God wanted, for that matter), there would still be others who were frustrated because our will was always being done. And not everything we want is good for us or God's world.

Clearly, failure to gain our every dream or hope has little to do with our faith, or the number of times we plead. The tears of frustration we shed lead us squarely into the reality that, in this world, we will not get all that we want or deserve. Justice is not perfect in this fallible world, and God's will is not realized in many instances. (Recall the prayer Jesus taught us: "Thy kingdom come, thy will be done.") In fact, frustration is our regular lot in this unpredictable and imperfect human life.

In experiencing frustration and disappointment, we join the ranks of God's faithful in Scripture and Christian history over the centuries. Our frustration, in fact, introduces us to the reality that we will not always get what we want in this life.

Give Up or Keep Trying and Waiting?

Some of us have learned that strong faith brings quick answers. But the biblical evidence is to the contrary. Israel waits for her redemption, Job waits for his redeemer, and Paul waits for a second coming that lingers generations later. The fact is that some things for which we ask take time. After all, the gift of a Promised Land took centuries to be delivered. A careful reading of the Book of Judges reminds us that all the promised land was never conquered.

How can we know if we have abandoned our hopes too early? Frustration and discouragement take their toll, and we may feel defeated and give up on our dreams—just when we should hold on to them. Jacob worked seven years for Rachel, and then was told he would receive Leah as a wife. He would have to work an additional seven years to receive Rachel. He chose to work the additional years.

Sometimes we face similar disappointments. We hope, dream, and work hard for our dreams, but we come up short. What then? Tears of frustration signal our first encounter with reality, with the fact that some things we want take hard work and a great deal of time. We flinch and wither at the discouraging news that we must further wait for what we desire. We sense that what we hoped for may never happen. Gradually, we face the probability that our dream will never occur.

Tears of frustration give us an opportunity to measure our capacity to continue nurturing certain hopes. We have the right to hold onto any dream that is dear to us, and we have the right to pay the price to continue the pursuit of our dreams. We alone can determine whether we have the energy and love to persist in the pursuit of a difficult dream. Tears of frustration remind us to evaluate long-held hopes and fervent dreams to make sure that we recognize the price of continued pursuit.

Some hopes and dreams are unrealistic. As the Apostle Paul stated in his letter to the Corinthian church, we must come to the place in our life when we give up childish dreams and embrace the realistic dreams of adulthood: "When I was a child I spoke as a child, I thought as a child, I reasoned as a child; when I became a man, I gave up childish ways." The capacity to evaluate important goals and dreams, assess their ongoing contributions to our lives, and the capacity to let go of those that no longer fit us are difficult but important steps to personal development.

How do we know when a dream should be relinquished? We must take careful account of how consistent our dream is with who we are—our gifts, skills, and identity as a person. We must evaluate the reasons our dreams have not materialized in the past, and accept the possibility that some dreams were never meant to be. We must assess whether we have the energy, the motivation, and the freedom to continue their pursuit.

We may even discover that certain dreams are not meant to be realized, but pursued. The value of these dreams is found in their ability to push us to the next chapter or challenge in our lives. Moses lived for years with the dream that he would enter the Promised Land; but the result of his dream was to make him a leader and guide to people in the wilderness.

This new perspective on hopes and dreams affects how we interpret God's role in our dreams and frustrations. Can a loving God care for us, understand our needs, and not grant us our requests? Certainly. As stated earlier, God does not grant every request. Some of our requests are not possible; others are not in our best interest. We may need to wait to understand. God sometimes does not grant us our wants because they are childhood fantasies that were never meant to be. Furthermore, God some-times does not grant us our dreams and hopes because they may be secondary to a more important process and purpose that we cannot understand until we shed tears of frustration.

In the meantime, we can remember that God understands our frustration and that our anger often is the processing of our grief over a loved fantasy that must be surrendered. The God of love and grace understands the journey our struggle must take before we can claim peace of mind.

Each of us probably remembers feeling relieved that some of our prayerful wishes were not granted. Thus, our frustration may be a chance to take another look at a cherished dream. Tears of frustration may introduce a waiting period that brings greater perspective to our wants. Perhaps we have not asked wisely. Perhaps we need to take careful stock of what we really need to dream and learn to dream better. Even in the pain of postponing heartfelt wishes we may discover a better hope or higher satisfaction while we wait.

Letting Go

If crying tears of frustration is our first movement in the journey of learning our limitations, a second part is giving ourselves per-mission to let go, even if reluctantly. No significant hope needs to be surrendered quickly. Tears of frustration assist in the impor-tant process of understanding resistance as a stage in growth.

The process of laying a dream to rest takes several steps. Tears are an important part of those steps; it helps to cry as often as nec-essary. With our tears, we flush out our helplessness and reluc-tance in surrendering long-cherished dreams. We cry not because we are "childish," but because our frustration is a reflec-tion of the value in which we held our surrendered dream.

We may need to voice our bitter disappointment at not real-izing our hopes and dreams. People honor us by listening to our disappointment at having to give up certain hopes and dreams. Those who neither chide us for crying, nor rush us to move on before we are ready to let go help us the most.

Fading hopes and dying expectations are experiences that grieve us. We naturally respond to such loss with the emptiness and sorrow that accompany other grief. Our process is one of letting go; it is the death of a dream. As with other grief, this letting go takes time. We may first deny the necessity of letting go and struggle with the fantasy that we can retain our dreams. We may also bargain with God and ourselves to keep dreams alive. We may become angry for having to give up something about which we care deeply. But step by step, we gradually release our hold upon the dream, and accept the reality of its loss.

Between Dreams

Next we usually experience the wilderness of living between dreams — things we had believed in before have died. We may be reluctant to dream again. Understandably bitter at the loss of valued goals, we pull back emotionally to protect ourselves. We may choose to live on the margin of personal involvement because we fear the pain of hoping and being disappointed again.

Motivation and excitement are naturally low after we let go of hopes and dreams. It is not necessary to tire ourselves trying to "pump" ourselves up. There will be time for a renewed sense of focus; we will set new goals; there will be new hopes — but not now — not immediately after letting go.

As children of God the dreamer, all of us need dreams. We come to worship, like Jacob to a Betel sanctuary, empty of dreams and hoping for new ones. But we also may be afraid of finding new dreams. We need to take our need to recover from loss seriously. Only then can we dream again. People who have loved and lost understand us. Friends help us most who listen patiently and give us time to linger. We need these people and this time to recover.

We may also become so discouraged that we make a pact with ourselves never to dream again. Painful as the loss of a long-held dream is, we may decide not to dream or hope again to avoid the pain we've just experienced in our recent loss. Only time can tell us whether our interim experience is a healing journey or stagnation. Somewhere on this journey, the pain of loss diminishes and we dare to dream again.

Dreaming Again

I listened as this fine, gifted couple stopped to tell me of their adoption plans. In fact, they had adopted before, but the promise of this bright, gentle child adopted ten years before had suddenly dissipated with a mysterious infection. Within two years, despite every treatment, the infection took her life. The tragedy of this loss of life, hopes, and dreams was frustrated further by the mysterious nature of the disease. The parents, who risked a great deal in adopting, were left disillusioned and vulnerable by the death.

But now, two years later, they sat in my office prepared to travel overseas, spend a large amount of money, and take a new risk with another child. How could they do this? From where did they draw their courage? What source of faith sustained them? How had they worked through their fears and hopes?

Life is regularly a miracle, interrupted by distractions of routine. In front of me sat a couple who had experienced what most professionals call the gravest of losses—the death of a child. They had already struggled with an unjust world where children are not always born to deserving parents. With every reason not to risk a dream of such magnitude again, here they were, ready to dream again. How did they do it?

By the grace of God they dreamed. Sustained in their loss from grief to frustration to resignation to healing, they had arrived at a clearing where they dared to dream again. The hopes they had held—and lost—were too big and too important to release permanently. They were at God's door, knocking again, and claiming the right to dream boldly.

By the grace of God all of us dream first because we are dreamers like God. Made in the image of the great dreamer, we do what our Maker did and continues to do. We weave dreams, we imagine, we hope, and we expect. We hurt at the loss of any major dream or hope. We struggle and declaim the injustice in this world that sometimes robs us of our fondest dreams. We dwell in frustration; we go home and grieve our losses. We wait and, in time, we "catch our spiritual breath."

And then we dream again. We dream again because we are creatures of hope and new horizons, like our Maker, who calls us out of the tombs to dream anew. We dream because our lives are empty without dreams to pursue. We no longer dream with the naive notion that we control everything or can do anything; instead, we dream with clear conviction that our frustrations with things not realized are measures of our determination to dream well; of the hard work we are willing to do for dreams; of the faith we have in our dreams. Tears of frustration, then, can be the mother of new-found determination and strong evidence of the passion within us to be faithful to our highest potential.

Chapter 7

---•---

Tears of Gratitude

My sudden, copious tears stumble out,
like words, trying to say what,
felt within, cannot be contained;
I have been graced!
And so I cry.

HELD CAPTIVE FOR ALMOST FIVE YEARS, he strained to focus on the memory of his loved ones' faces. From a distance he saw the small figure of a woman coming toward him in the dim morning of that winter dawn on the outskirts of Beirut. How many times had he been told that his wife had died? How many times had she been told that he was dead? Had the children grown so much he wouldn't even recognize them? Strange irony that nearly five years ago he had gone to negotiate the release of others but was himself taken prisoner. And was he actually being released? Every step toward that woman seemed to strengthen hope.

Then he finally reached her. The gentle, loving face of his wife was unmistakable even through his weary, swollen eyelids. He took her in his arms; she folded her arms around him. Neither of them spoke. There were only tears. Terry Anderson could not understand his inability to speak. He had rehearsed this moment many times during the loneliness of his abduction. But now there were no words. No words, that is, except the eloquent, flowing language of tears.

We have all been afraid to hope for good news when bad news has dismembered our safety. We hold our feelings in check and expect only the worst. We do what we can to cope with the shock of change. We tell ourselves that we can face whatever has happened. Traumatized by destructive crises, we hope against hope that our greatest fears will not be realized and that we will find relief from our trauma.

If good news intervenes after bad news has controlled us, we may shed tears of gratitude. These tears often surprise us, suddenly expelling our anxiety, loss, and vulnerability from deep within us. Just as suddenly as we encounter tragedy, we experience a glimmer of hope. Now, taking little for granted, we cry tears of gladness.

We all experience tears of joy during our lives, sometimes under extreme circumstances. The mother holds her breath until she sees her son safely pulled from an overturned car—and begins to cry. The father of a soldier, reunited with his son after months of separation, cries upon his son's safe return. After surgery to remove a tumor, the anxious cancer patient learns from her doctor that the tumor was benign—and cries tears of gratitude.

Why do we cry tears of gratitude? In the midst of many negative surprises in life, there are some unexpected tragedies that shake us to the core. When surprised by trauma and disaster, we brace ourselves, bridle our hopes, and often fear the worst.

Stunning events occur so rapidly that we barely have time to catch our breath or recover our balance. Shock and numbness usually delay our first responses to negative surprises. We repress our feelings, stacking and storing them up inside of us, and wait for a time when we feel comfortable facing them.

Tears of gratitude are delayed celebrations after very stressful events. They confirm the fact that things did not turn out as badly as we feared, that something good has balanced something bad. Tears of gratitude, then, usually come at the end of profound tension, when we receive relief from stress and discover a new sense of hope.

Taking Good for Granted

Most of us are not ungrateful people. We live in a society and a time that provides many comforts. We are probably the healthiest group of humans ever to live. Most of us have the belief that if we act responsibly, work hard, and lead decent lives, we should live graciously and in peace.

We have come to take comfort, health, and peace for granted. But accidents, disasters, and personal tragedies do occur, and they are startling interruptions in our usually comfortable and peaceful lives. Destructive events jeopardize the delicate balance of our lives, and we experience disorientation, anxiety, and despair.

How Traumatic Surprises Affect Us

Stunned by changes that upset or harm our well-being, we become anxious, lose perspective, and focus on our losses. Unexpected destructive events traumatize us because they rob us of something or someone very dear to us. Common traumatic events often include accidents, disaster, and disease.

Accidents

Back from a Friday night football game at which their daughter, Maureen, had led the cheers, the Daltons were getting ready for bed. The telephone rang. Maureen had been in a car accident and was in critical condition. An only child, she had been the object of most of their affection and hopes. Now she was hovering on the brink of death. Everything else in their life seemed distant and unimportant.

The Daltons camped out at the hospital on a four-day vigil while Maureen remained in a coma. The doctors had given her only a small chance to survive and had warned that if she did live, there could be major damage to her brain. On the fifth day, Maureen opened her eyes and recognized her mother. She couldn't speak, nor was there any indication how extensively her brain might be damaged. But the thrill of looking into her daughter's eyes—seeing her recognition—brought tears to her mother's eyes. "She's alive!" Mrs. Dalton exclaimed, "and that's all that matters to me right now. She's alive. I thought I'd lost her."

Accidents that harm us or our loved ones change our lives dramatically. They often change the priorities in our lives; what we once felt was important is unexpectedly abandoned in favor of responding to an immediate need or crisis. When accidents occur to people we love, we turn our energies and attention to their care. We abandon our routines to respond quickly to the demands of a crisis.

Accidents also throw us off balance. They catch us off guard and force us to live with the anxiety and the unknown. We sense we can no longer provide safety for ourselves or for someone dear to us. This sense of losing control can be traumatizing.

Disaster

The news that a middle school student had shot and killed several classmates brought panic and fear to a small community in one state. Parents, teachers, and students rushed to the school grounds, each hoping desperately that someone they loved had not been hurt. Dazed by the sudden fear that their child might have been killed, tearful and traumatized parents ran from child to child. One minute they were relieved that a neighbor's child was safe, the next minute they were anxious, wanting to find their own loved ones. At the sight of their own flesh and blood, parents engulfed their children in their arms and wept tears of gratitude.

Like other tragedies, disasters redirect our energies and make us focus on immediate needs. The unexpected harm causes us anxiety and tension. Such calamities also throw us off balance. In the aftermath of disaster, we struggle to regain perspective and peace of mind.

Disease

Any medical condition that becomes life-threatening generates a new set of issues for us and for our families. Some diseases are so traumatic that the mere mention of them disturbs us. The word cancer and its implications of suffering and death, for example, has the capacity to create profound anxiety. The fragile nature of life is exposed when words such as cancer are spoken.

The family, gathered in the conference room to hear the doctor's diagnosis. They were anxious and clung to each word the doctor said: "We need to do surgery right away, in order to stop the internal bleeding. What we don't know is whether she can stand surgery at her age and condition. She could die on the operating table. But if we don't perform the surgery, I fear she may not make it either." The reality of her condition was sudden, sharp, and devastating.

Many of us listen helplessly to the news that our loved ones are slowly dying. We grasp for hope and long for news our loved ones will be healed. In cases where healing is not possible, we want those we hold dear to be free of pain. But sometimes neither is possible.

When we feel unable to help those we love, there is distress. We try gently and patiently to tend to our loved ones during their painful journeys toward death, while we often struggle with hiding our inner turmoil.

Tears of Gladness

Unbelievable as it may seem, there is occasion to shed tears of gladness and gratitude during times of trauma. Consumed by ongoing and joy-depriving tragedy, we are sometimes surprised by unexpected hopes and we cry tears of gratitude. These tears are born of relief, a new sense that not all is lost. They are created by the sudden realization that there are things to celebrate in the midst of our agony. These tears are driven by an internal impulse of gratitude for the sudden recognition of good and grace despite tragedy.

Our tears of gratitude are a celebration that hope and joy can also surprise us. The mother and father whose daughter lies comatose and possibly dying are buoyed by the hope that she has awakened. Even if she is forever changed, they realize they may have a second chance at life with their daughter. Having rehearsed the frightening thought of her death, they cry for joy at having her back.

A schoolgirl's parent sheds tears of gladness the moment she lays eyes on her daughter, safe despite the playground shooting. This parent, too, had rehearsed the worst possible outcome, but is now grateful because her daughter is alive.

Tears of gladness also come to those who recognize relief when it comes to suffering loved ones. Consider the son who watches his father's last breath of air but is grateful that his father is free of the suffering that had controlled his life for years.

Tears of relief at death are not a celebration of someone's death. Rather, they indicate the welcomed fact that someone loved no longer hurts. We wished them relief—sometimes wondering how they could stand the agony. We felt helpless with the little comfort we could offer. But now, hurtful as it is, death offers the merciful gift of relief.

I remember the words of a friend whose eleven-year-old daughter suffered with a brutal leukemic condition. He described the anguish he felt from watching her hurt for hours. He sometimes had to place a washcloth between her teeth so she could bite down against unbearable pain. When death finally came, he saw it as a welcome ally of his child, and he shed tears of gratitude for the relief it gave her.

That is why as a minister at funerals I've hastened to remind family members that any feelings of relief they feel do not contradict their love. The relief we feel for those who once hurt but have died is that we know they now sleep peacefully in the healing arms of God. We celebrate their freedom from all life's fragile constraints.

When my father died of Alzheimer's at age eighty-five, I was relieved for him. As the disease progressed, the man I once knew changed before my eyes. He slowly lost the ability to use his human gifts as his once keen mind succumbed to the disease. Only pain and sorrow were left in his life. It was time to go, time for the relief of pain he did not deserve. I was also relieved for my mother, whose covenant with my father would have driven her to an early death caring for him. I shed tears of grief when he died—but I also shed tears of gratitude.

I still love my father, and I miss him. But we are called in this fallible world to embrace the gift of life and to release it. As believers, we are strengthened by the sure hope of resurrection.

Goodness for Which We Dared Not Hope

Sometimes in the midst of tragedy we celebrate the good in life with tears. We watch a film in which an almost vanquished hero rises up against all odds and triumphs, and we respond with passionate tears of joy at the achievement. Because we are capable of being moved emotionally by a make-believe story, it should not surprise us when we are stirred to tears by life's surprising, positive moments.

Just a few years ago, a Philadelphia newspaper carried a story of a young girl separated from her twin sister and family during the Nazis' occupation of Europe during World War II. After surviving two concentration camps and unsuccessfully searching for family survivors, the girl traveled to the United States. Years later, having restructured her life in America, she read a reporter's interview of an orphan survivor of the Holocaust in an Israeli magazine. To the Jewish-American woman's surprise, the survivor's story detailed events that could only be known by a member of her own family. She wrote to the magazine and eventually confirmed that the survivor was her sister, now living in Israel.

The sisters corresponded, and the American sister invited her Israeli twin to visit her in Pennsylvania, forty-seven years after they were separated on another continent.

The Philadelphia newspaper that first printed the story followed the potential family reunion. On the day the European sister arrived at the Philadelphia airport, an eager crowd of the paper's readers gathered to witness the reunion. A television camera caught the twins as they caught sight of one another at the airport terminal. The two women increased their pace, running into each other's arms. Both sisters cried at the embrace and, when they turned around to face the crowd, all the people had tears in their eyes. An entire audience shared their tears of gratitude that day.

Such rare human dramas naturally cause tears of gratitude. But we also experience situations in our lives that evoke our tears of gratitude, and these tears of joy need to be understood. We cry tears of joy out of an overflow of feelings we have. We feel pain at a loss and a healing gladness over grace. We feel anger at being helpless and restorative joy in being nurtured in our helplessness. During a worship service, we may be saddened one moment and then cry tears of celebration the next. We can be overcome by news of tragedy at a family event, and then cry tears of gladness over a good surprise.

Those of us who cry tears of gratitude must sometimes help friends who have been consoling us during tragic events understand these new tears. Some of us have been "prompted" over the years to respond to tears by assuming they are always evidence of bad news. If we have been openly shedding tears of frustration, pain, or sorrow, we may need to interpret our tears of gratitude so their language can be understood by those who love us most.

Grace has always been God's gift to us at broken places. We need only look to Jesus Christ who came to show us the face of a glad God. A God who throws a party for a prodigal once in crisis, but now safe. Jesus tells the story of a shepherd God who invites friends to celebrate the finding of a lost animal; and who calls neighbors to celebrate the recovery of a lost memento.

Tears of gratitude mirror the humble response of a tender heart that has been surprised by grace during a tragic event. May glad tears flow; they are a keen reminder that we have been surprised by something good in life when we least expected it. We are declaring that we recognize grace when we receive it, and that we are deeply moved by its importance. Our tears of grace are an emotional bond with a compassionate Maker who creates grace in the worst of times!

Chapter 8

—•—

Tears of Loneliness

*As I sit alone, I try to remember
how many times he sat alone—wishing
for a companion in his isolation,
wondering if anybody cared.*

I WAS SEVENTEEN AND EAGER TO BEGIN that first day of college. My parents, missionaries to Brazil, had traveled with me to Texas, placed me in the barracks dorm room where I was assigned, and driven away. As they left, the excitement and commotion of being in a new place still distracted me. I had already walked to the campus bookstore and bought my books. I remember standing there amongst a sea of strangers, listening to people greet each other in a Texas accent still unfamiliar to me. I was suddenly overcome by the powerful sensation of feeling very far away from anyone I knew or anyone who cared about me.

I walked back to the silence of my empty room, crawled up on my bed, and hid muffled tears in my pillow. I had never felt so lonely in my life.

When do the tears of loneliness appear? They come to us when we miss the encouraging presence of a loved one who reminded us that we mattered, that we belonged. God made us for fellowship, and all of us have a deep need to connect with other human beings. We hurt when we feel disconnected. God placed us in families, intimate friendships, and in larger communities, so that we could commune with one another—and with God. Sometimes we cry when we feel far away from those who love us, when we feel forgotten, abandoned, or misunderstood.

Counselors remind us that all of us were created with certain legitimate needs: We need attention, acceptance, appreciation, encouragement, affection, support, respect, security, and belonging. When some of these needs are met during childhood, they become lasting gifts to our self-image. When some of these needs go unmet, we hunger for their fulfillment and long for people who will offer them to us. Loneliness is an internal cry of absence, the loss of some nurturing element important to our life.

She leaned back slightly for a moment in the chair, gazing out my window at the family of five making their way through the parking lot. I followed her pain-filled gaze first to the family, laughing as they walked, then back to her, her eyes filled with tears.

"Tonight," she explained, "I'll go back to an empty house. No one will call. I'll prepare a meal just for myself, sit and eat, watch a program on TV, and fall asleep in that chair, afraid that I will wake up before dawn. And if I do wake, I'll walk into that lonely, empty bedroom and go to sleep all by myself. And if should I die, I know no one will miss me for a while."

The tears of loneliness are far more common than we think. We seen them in the eyes of busy people, trying to shove aside the emptiness they feel inside. We hear them in the poignant sobbing of those isolated from their loved ones. We understand they are in the unhappy voices of those surrounded by others, but who cannot find anyone who cares about them, knows them, or understands them.

Being lonely is not the same as being alone. All of us need privacy and space. We need time to be with others and time to be by ourselves. It is important to be alone sometimes. We can only have a proper sense of worth (a self we like) if we have time for ourselves apart from anyone else. It is possible to be alone and not feel lonely. We are alone and fulfilled when our needs are being met while by ourselves. We feel lonely when a deep need inside of us is not being met.

Why is it that sometimes we can be alone and content, and at other times, we can be in a crowd of people and feel lonely? The answer, in part, has to do with our needs and whether or not they are being met.

Alone and Content

There are times when we need to be alone. Paul Tournier, a Christian therapist, reminds us that a part of us can be nurtured and developed only when we are by ourselves. We become a person with our own thoughts, feelings, and personal identity only when we know ourselves apart from anyone else. That is why as children we began to push away from our parents. In order to be a unique and fully developed person, we must separate even from those we most identify with and deeply love.

Child development experts tell us that an infant only begins to understand herself separately from her mother during her second year of life. We declare our autonomy as independent human beings by asserting the word "no" to parents or other caregivers. The assertion is not a statement indicating rejection of another person; it is a clear declaration of knowing we possess our own thoughts and feelings. The infant's cry of resistance is actually a God-given declaration that we know ourselves as a person with a separate identity.

Having a heart and mind of our own is essential to being a person. We can give ourselves to other human beings only if we are distinct persons ourselves. God designed us to become independent of our parents. God created us to have minds of our own in our relationships with him. In order to develop this wonderful gift of selfhood, we need time alone to discover our own thoughts, to understand our own uniqueness, and to celebrate God's gift of individuality in us. Developing the capacity to become separate selves, to become distinct human beings who can love, relate, and bond with others, is part of our living homework.

Even in marriage, the sense of being an individual person apart from another is essential. Though the Bible speaks of becoming one flesh in the covenant of marriage, it never suggests that we give up our selfhood in becoming one. As Ruth Bell Graham has aptly assessed, if both partners in a marriage think alike and agree on everything, one of them is unnecessary.

Being alone is also important for the development of our self-esteem. We learn to like ourselves to the degree that we spend time understanding ourselves. Reflection and self-study are important exercises in self-appreciation. The child who spends some time playing and working by herself, for example, is learning to appreciate herself and celebrate her own capacity to think, imagine, create, and feel uniquely.

Feeling Lonely

Loneliness is an unpleasant experience. It is contrary to the fulfilling experience of affirming our selfhood through the developmental time we spend alone. To feel lonely is to sense the absence of someone we miss. Loneliness is all the feelings of separation, absence, and emptiness.

How can we manage the tears of loneliness? Our first challenge is to recognize when we are lonely to determine if the tears we shed actually are tears of loneliness. The second step is to identify the specific needs within us that cry out for fulfillment. Our third task is to structure ways to appropriately meet those needs and reduce our loneliness. Fourth, we must identify the needs within us that cannot be met and learn the discipline of living with those limitations.

Recognizing Loneliness

The tears of loneliness may catch us unexpectedly in public places or during what seem to be pleasant moods. We need to look within for the subtle, internal promptings that signify the void we feel. What am I missing that has made me unhappy?

A challenge with loneliness is that its painful affects are so easily mistaken for grief. With grief, the focus is usually specific: We mourn the loss of an individual who has died or left us. Loneliness can include grief, for it involves the realization that we feel cut off from important people in our lives. But it is typically a general sense of distance from all those who matter to us, coupled with a sense of distance from ourselves.

He was twelve years old. He had been arrested with three other boys for shoplifting in a downtown mall and brought that same day to the Children's Center where I served as Chaplain. He walked slowly into that noisy detention room of more than twenty children. Once in the room, his eyes searched for a quiet corner. Seeing one, he moved toward it with the casual look of someone who had no particular purpose. When he found a dark, hidden spot, he curled up in it, lowered his head, and silently began to cry.

His buddies, except for one, had all been released to their parents hours before. Orphaned at eight, kept by a crippled grandmother, he knew no one would claim him that weekend. He wiped the tears with his dirty shirt and stared aimlessly out the window.

I watched him out of the corner of my eye as I talked to another boy. When I walked up to him, I leaned down to shield him from curious eyes and called him by name. The surprise of hearing me use his name startled him. He looked up at me, eyes overflowing. Rarely had I seen a face look lonelier than his.

"Been here long?" I asked, trying to look gently but directly into his eyes. He shook his head. "It's a long way from your own bed, and sometimes it can be very lonely. . . . Is there anything I can do for you?" He gazed at me, as if trying to figure out who I was. "I'm the chaplain here, Bobby; that's like a pastor or priest outside. I've come to see how you're doing and to see what I can do for you before I leave tonight."

"I'm not sure my grandmother knows where I am. . . . She worries about me."

"They usually call family to tell them where you are," I replied.

"But she doesn't—we don't have a phone, " he explained.

"Does someone else you know have a phone that I can call, so they will tell your grandmother where you are?" His face looked more alert, and he told me that a neighbor down the street often passed on messages to his family. He stumbled trying to remember the phone number, but got it right after a few tries.

"She hasn't been alone for years. . . . I know she's scared." His eyes swelled up again with tears, and he lowered his head to hide them. I told him I would call her and tell her where he was. Then, for his benefit, I said I would tell her that he might be detained for several days.

I asked him if anything else was on his mind. He shook his head and swallowed a lump in his throat. So I asked him if I could pray with him privately and for what I might pray. He said yes, and shrugged his shoulders. Then he asked that his grandmother be remembered. I prayed:

> Dear God, you know that Bobby is concerned for his grandmother and wishes he could be with her—but not here. You also know how scary and lonely this place can be and how far away Bobby is from anyone he trusts. Care for him—he doesn't know what to ask for. Help him through the night. Care for his grandmother and give her peace of mind away from him. Give him peace of mind, too, and quiet his fears so he can sleep. Give him courage and patience, and help him through this nightmare. Help him know you care.

Few of us have experienced being in jail—but almost all of us have felt as Bobby did. We all have memories of tears shed in the loneliness of a very impersonal world. But we don't always identify the experience as loneliness. One of the first symptoms of loneliness is an internal sense of alienation from people and our surroundings. We feel at odds with, and distant from, those around us. We feel an unpleasant dissatisfaction with life as it is, and we withdraw emotionally from those around us. We begin to tell ourselves that we are disconnected from anyone we know, and we experience a deep sadness.

When lonely, we feel a void inside because we feel very unfulfilled and restless. We may become depressed, find little meaning in life, or have the motivation to do much. We may weep for no apparent reason. Detached and listless, we feel separated and isolated from people; we doubt that anyone really cares about us.

Perhaps the most important thing we need to understand about loneliness is that the feeling has to do both with how we read our relationship to others and how we feel about ourselves, regardless of the presence of other people. Many of us believe we are lonely because we are by ourselves. But we also know that we can be with a number of people and still feel lonely.

Loneliness while among others means that the feeling is not simply a matter of being by ourselves. Loneliness comes when we don't feel connected with people, when we don't feel people understand us as unique, or when we feel people don't care about us. Loneliness is the absence of connection with anyone and the feeling of being separated from those with whom we seek a bond.

Loneliness is our reaction to having failed to find someone with whom we can be known and accepted at the deepest levels of our being. All of us have a need to be intimately involved with another human being—not so much sexually, but emotionally, psychically, and spiritually. Lonely people are people who are struggling to be connected with others.

Identifying Our Needs in Loneliness

Tears of loneliness are a sign that our community of support has been altered. To feel lonely means to be aware that people who value us (and whom we value) are not available to meet our needs for affirmation and importance. We therefore feel less important and less valuable. Our self-esteem suffers.

To be considered important by someone else is not a matter of arrogance or pride; it is a matter of worth and validation. If someone thinks we are important, they are saying that we matter to them. People who value us help us develop self-worth.

In addition, if no one around us relates to us in a meaningful way, we feel disconnected from those around us; we feel we do not belong to them (are not related), and we are not engaged with them (part of them). Loneliness is the perception that we are not a part of other people's lives.

Detached from other people, we feel distant from them. We resent this disconnection from community and develop feelings of alienation. We tell ourselves that they do not understand us, that we are all alone, that no one cares about us, and that we are not important. Our disenchantment with others creates more distance from them, and we begin to feel abandoned—left on our own. Alienation creates a wall of isolation that separates us from affection, nurture, and belonging.

The alienation we feel is a suspicion that we really do not matter. Loneliness is an alienation from ourselves, from others, and from our sense of purpose. What we are missing is our need to be of some value to ourselves, to others, and to what we believe in; we feel disconnected from all three.

To quell our tears of loneliness, then, we must address our deepest needs for purpose, value, and affinity. We gain meaning by recognizing that we belong to a network of relationships to which we make a difference. We gain purpose by believing that we are part of a valuable design larger than our individual lives. We gain value by choosing to see ourselves as worthy and significant human beings who are capable both of being loved and of loving someone else.

Tears of loneliness invite us to both pain and opportunity. The pain we may share is the discomfort of losing our "safe" isolation, as well as the accountability of living with responsibility to relationships and to the values we hold dear. The opportunity is a chance to see ourselves as valuable, to discover a community to which we belong, and to discover our purpose and value in life.

By recognizing the opportunities tears of loneliness afford us, we come closer to satisfying our basic needs. But we must go further and learn how to get our basic needs met so that loneliness ceases to control us.

Meeting Basic Needs

Our third task in challenging loneliness is finding ways to meet some fundamental needs. We can make choices and changes in our daily routines to meet several of the untended needs that produced our loneliness.

But we may face one personal barrier to meeting some of our needs—our assessment that our needs are not legitimate. If we decide that as adults we no longer need attention, affection, or affirmation, we will have a hard time convincing ourselves to meet those needs. If we consider it childish to need attention, for example, we will spend little time finding ways to meet that need. If we interpret affection or affirmation as luxuries, we will expend little effort in trying to satisfy them.

We may need only ask ourselves several questions to determine if our thinking is faulty, hindering us from meeting our needs: Is my human need for attention appropriate? Is wanting the interest of another person legitimate? As adults, do we need nurture, support, or care from others? Is the need for affection and affirmation appropriate for adults? The answer to these questions is, of course, yes. All of us deserve attention and care. But if we struggle with the idea that we have the right to certain feelings and needs, then our progress is hindered.

Hopefully, we have already determined that we too have emotional rights as adults. If we are not convinced that we do, then perhaps we can learn something from Jesus Christ himself, who took his own needs seriously. He once took three disciples with him to Gethsemane, because he did not want to be alone during an overnight ordeal. Earlier, he admonished his disciples for chastising a woman who spent rich perfume on him, declaring that "she had done a good thing" in one of the loneliest weeks of his ministry (passion week, when most of his friends abandoned him). He even made sure that his mother and a close friend had each other as companions during their mutual grief.

We shed tears of loneliness because we are deprived of attention and care in our daily routine. Many of us have trouble asking people for attention or requesting nurture when we need someone to listen to us. As a result, we live feeling lonely and isolated. We may have many acquaintances, but few people who truly care about us. We need to give ourselves permission to need the attention and focus of nurturing relationships.

Choosing friends is not an easy task. We know that no one can pick our friends for us; but we often leave friendships and relationships to chance or accident. We tend to hope that meaningful relationships will appear, but we wait, passively, for someone else to find us. The relationships and friendships that will meet our needs are very unlikely to just happen. We need to spend time intentionally seeking out relationships to meet our needs. Only then can we overcome loneliness.

What are we looking for in relationships? First of all, assuming that most of us have family living geographically away from us, we are looking for a few people who can be nurturing and caring of us in a familial way. What does that mean? Our family of origin assumed that we needed some attention, some care, and some nurturing. Although away from most family sources of care, such needs must still be met.

In relationships, we need people who are willing to spend time with us and give us their full attention. We need relationships with people who consider us important enough to care for us, who inquire about our welfare, who are interested in our joys and pains. We want people who understand us and who receive us as we are. We need people who value us and respect us, and who take initiative to draw us out. We need people to whom we are safe telling our secrets, and a few folks who encourage us and cheer us on. All these needs are legitimate, and we need them met in specific relationships. How do we go about choosing such soul mates?

Taking Initiative

To find significant relationships, we need to look for them. To do so, we must attend social gatherings where people holding values and interests similar to ours are likely to gather. We need to meet people in a variety of social settings that by design bring people like us together. Civic activities, religious gatherings, and charity projects are examples of events where people gather with common goals and hopes.

We may choose a variety of social activities, but we must understand that we are more likely to meet people with whom we have much in common at a social activity in keeping with our lifestyles and priorities. We may meet a number of lonely people seeking a relationship in a bar during happy hour, but the chance that any of them are seeking a long-term, trusting, vulnerable, responsible, and deep relationship is limited.

For that same reason, short-term sexual encounters fail to produce the kind of intimacy we need. Designed to express the deepest of human connections physically, sexual intercourse between two people can affirm the most profound form of interconnection. The sexual act, however, does not create intimacy, but can only reflect a reality already felt by its participants. This produces painful loneliness that some people feel soon after a sexual interchange in which their lives and souls are not connected.

Exploring a Relationship

Our search for a sound relationship must always begin with caution and discernment. We must spend time assessing the compatibility of interests and depth in a relationship. Most of us have been trained to engage in shallow conversations that maintain distance. We exchange pleasantries, talk about light subjects, and listen for areas of commonality.

One of the first indications that we may be in a conversation with someone we want to get to know is when the other person asks us about ourselves and shows interest in our responses. We may look for certain characteristics. Does our conversationalist look at us when speaking or listening? Does he acknowledge what we say somehow by word or gesture? Does she invite more conversation by what she asks? When someone even repeats what we just said, we have a keen sense that he or she is taking us seriously—and receiving what we are saying.

Such first impressions can be deciding factors in whether or not we decide to pursue relationships. Whenever we find someone capable of expressing interest in us and taking initiative to establish or maintain a conversation, we are probably dealing with someone who is capable of nurture, care, and mutual responsibility in a relationship. These first signals offer us hope that we may find more in common with our potential friends.

Common ground and a stable sense that we can trust someone usually take us to a level of trust and risk. Having found an initial connection in our conversations, we may decide to try to reach more personal levels of disclosure and open ourselves to vulnerability.

Vulnerability

People who study communication tell us that in order to reach deeper and more satisfying levels in relationships, we need to share our thoughts, feelings, intentions, hopes, and wants. To achieve a level of trust in a relationship, we also want to take responsibility for our side of the friendship. To do so means that we are not only willing to disclose our thoughts and feelings to another, but that we begin the process by taking initiative ourselves.

Reaching deeper levels of trust and care means taking some risks by saying more about ourselves. We can only bond with others when we share the joys, fears, hopes, and passions that shape our life. When we reveal anything significant about ourselves, we risk being misunderstood, rejected, ridiculed, or ignored.

Each of those painful experiences has happened to us before, and we are cautious about letting someone else into our private lives. However, we cannot live on a superficial basis with everyone. We must risk parts of our deeper selves with others in order to feel connected in meaningful ways.

We do not open ourselves to others automatically. We want to know that we will be treated well. We want assurance our private truths treated responsibly. We want (deserve) to have our secrets held sacred. Vulnerability is a continuous experiment. We develop it gradually. Our trust must be earned. But the trust of others also must be earned. We seek a few people who also choose us, those who want a relationships of depth and compassion because they value us as unique friends.

Continuity

We regularly need food, shelter, and rest. But we also need a regular "diet" of nurture, affirmation, and attention. We need a few good people in our lives. They help us receive steady interpersonal sustenance, including encouragement, support, and care. One way to ensure we have a regular supply of these necessities is to plan small, informal, and consistent contacts with supportive people.

There are many ways to structure meaningful relationships so that they provide us regular strength for the daily journey. We can schedule lunch weekly with a special friend, share a cup of coffee with three colleagues every other week, take a Saturday morning walk with a chosen friend, arrange a telephone hour reserved for a long-distance friend, and so on. The point is to take action, to reach out and make human contacts that feed us emotionally and spiritually on a regular basis.

Learning to Like Ourselves

What part does not liking ourselves play in our loneliness? Does our self-esteem have anything to do with it? Most of us who counsel lonely people can verify that how we feel about ourselves plays an important role in our sense of isolation and longing. How can we change that? How can we learn to like ourselves so that loneliness doesn't control us?

Learning to like ourselves as children was a job our parents had a lot to do with because, if they liked us, we would probably like ourselves. But learning to like ourselves as adults is our job, and the sooner we learn to do it, the less lonely we will be—even when we're alone. We must learn to value ourselves as persons who have something to contribute to the world. Even when no one else is reminding us of our worth, we should be able to love ourselves. How do we learn to like ourselves?

We learn to like ourselves as worthwhile persons by taking notice of our abilities, characteristics, and capacities. Robinson Crusoe, Daniel Defoe's hero in the novel of the same name, learned to live on a lonely island alone for nearly 25 years, and then with only one companion, Friday. (Despite the presence of Friday, Crusoe remained somewhat isolated because of his own prejudices and the two men's cultural differences.) How did Crusoe survive? Besides using his imagination and hard labor to find food and shelter, Crusoe learned to spend time taking stock of himself and his assets. We rarely do that.

Defoe's character was based upon a real person's life, John Selkirk, who survived a shipwreck and lived by himself for years on an island off Chile during the seventeenth century. Selkirk quickly discovered that he was by himself on the island and that he needed to rely on his own resources to survive. He worked every day to survive physically, then realized that his spirit also needed nourishment.

Like his real life counterpart, Crusoe began by taking himself seriously. He listened to his own thoughts, feelings, and hopes. He paid attention to his own imagination. He dreamed and tried out his dreams. He developed goals and purposes for himself. He gave himself standards and expectations. He discovered talents and skills and used them for his survival, entertainment, and enjoyment.

Have we learned to enjoy ourselves as persons? Robinson Crusoe invented conversations, engaging himself with self-dialog. He learned to laugh and amuse himself. He spent time examining his immediate world and discovered so much to learn and do that he put loneliness to flight.

We also need to learn how to live with ourselves, as well as how to be alone. Trapped at times on our own isolated islands, we have no control over the isolation and distance in which we live. But we do have control over what we do with ourselves. We can imagine ways to create, work, and entertain ourselves, much like Robinson Crusoe did. We can learn more about ourselves by spending time listening to ourselves. We can explore our capacities and skills (most of us rarely discover half the things we can do with our minds, hands, and heart). We can take charge of our isolation by fulfilling useful purposes and goals.

In real life, Crusoe's actions and behavior are what any counselor would recommend to a depressed, lonely person: Take stock of what you do have control over, celebrate what you can do, and get busy taking charge of the part of your life you can direct. Crusoe set goals, established expectations, and created purposes for his daily life. Giving life meaning is our responsibility.

When we begin to take charge of our lives, we begin to enjoy being with ourselves. Most of us have taken ourselves for granted for so long that we must get reacquainted with the stranger inside us. We can begin by discovering the world of possibilities in our imagination. There are many things we can create with our own mind and make with our own hands.

If we spend time discovering our capacities and skills, we will learn to value ourselves in a new way. So much of our low self-esteem comes from not knowing ourselves well. We need to spend time discovering and take the time to celebrate what we discover.

Meaning and Purpose

The third way we dispel loneliness is by developing a personal sense of meaning and purpose in life. Counselors describe us as a generation of people who choose to be entertained rather than engaged in a meaningful set of activities that give us purpose and direction. Yet once the distractions and amusements are finished, we must again face the emptiness of a life devoid of meaning and value.

How do purposes and causes alter loneliness? If we aspire to certain goals, we give ourselves reasons for living. We need causes that transcend our temptation to live only for ourselves. One of the struggles of loneliness is self-absorption. Theologian Martin Buber and others remind us that, as human beings, we need to focus on ourselves in relationship to someone and something else.

Each of us must choose our own causes. Making promises to purposes and issues outside ourselves returns us to the fact we are responsible for creating our own meaning and values in life. By choosing causes and issues ourselves, we affirm that happiness, joy, and meaning do not come from outside of us but are within us. We become less preoccupied with ourselves.

Accepting Limitations

Sometimes the people we know do not give us all we need. There may be people who mean well and want to care for us, but they may not offer us what we yearn for. How can we more effectively get what we need from the people around us?

An obvious answer is that sometimes people do not know what we need. The best help we can offer them (and ourselves) is to ask for what we need. We struggle with this simple procedure because we either think we shouldn't ask for certain things or we believe that asking for anything devalues the giving.

But these thoughts are not valid. First, we are entitled to attention and nurture, because we were made by God for communion. We have the right to connect and bond in meaningful ways. Second, we have legitimate needs. Our loved ones, however, cannot guess what we need. We can either help ourselves and them by telling them what we need, or we can go without getting our basic needs met—and grow increasingly frustrated and lonely. We who are willing to ask are more likely to get the attention and care we need.

Our needs may also go untended because those around us are incapable of meeting them. They may be needy themselves. Life may be making demands on them that prevents them from fulfilling our needs. They simply may not have the capacity to fulfill our needs. In such cases, we may have to accept these facts. We may have to broaden our search for capable relationships and people who are willing to enter deeper covenants of care with us.

We may also discover that some of our needs may be fulfilled only in the distant future. For example, some single people who seek marriage and children may have to wait before finding their right mates. Some children may have to wait until they are adults, until they have families of their own, before finding the familial love they desire. In these periods of waiting, the local church, as the "family of God," may meet some of our relational needs.

Physical Isolation and Loneliness

We must realize that distance from our networks of support does not mean we are cut off from others. We have more ways to establish and maintain relationships than people did in the past. If we are separated physically from our community of caring friends, we may need to maintain connection with them by telephone, letter, or e-mail.

We also can create new bonds and friendships when we move geographically. But this takes time. One way we can bridge the time between old and new nurturing relationships is to keep in touch with those we left behind. While we look for people in a local circle of care, we can be nurtured by those who already love us.

Such waiting periods are often our loneliest times. Having known what it is like to be connected to someone, we feel the sharp contrast of being out of contact with caring people. Times between friendships can be lonely journeys of the soul. We need patience and faith during such transitions. We need patience to endure the absence, awareness that we have bonded in the past, and faith that we will form lasting and worthwhile relationships again.

Loneliness, while unavoidable, need never be permanent. Armed with the assurance that we are someone valued and worth knowing, we renew our efforts to create new and lasting bonds in the next circle of relationships. Though we may shed tears of loneliness in the meantime, we can be assured we will dry our tears and focus on the rich potential of tomorrow's friendships. God closes no doors behind us without opening windows and doors before us.

Chapter 9

---•—•—•---

Tears of Manipulation

Yesterday I shed tears—to change your mind;
Today I wept, hoping you'd love me more;
Tomorrow if I cry—ask me why.

S HE TOOK THE SWITCH IN HER HANDS, her eyes focused and
squinting. Her children dared not move as they stared up at
their mother. "Every time that you disobey me, you hurt me"—
she paused, her eyes filled with tears, and she raised the switch
with her left hand— "just like this." She brought the switch
down on her other arm, over and over again, until red marks and
welts made everyone wince. "And every time you disobey me, I
want you to remember what you do to your mother, and how
much it hurts me."

I wanted to leave the room, a reluctant witness to a savage
whipping and a startling scene, but I was stuck in the corner. My
cousins took turns crying and grimacing. Their mother, proudly
displaying her abused arm as evidence of her pain, increased her
tears as she asked the children if they understood. They understood, all right. Because she had lost most other means of controlling their behavior, my aunt was trying to manipulate them with
shame and guilt. I will always remember the scene.

Why do we cry tears of manipulation? Persuasive tears help us gain control, acquire attention, secure sympathy, or protect ourselves. When we feel vulnerable and fragile, we may have learned to cry to evoke pity or compassion in those who might hurt us. When we fail to get a desired result, we may resort to tears to get what we want. When we feel out of control, we may use tears to regain our balance or some degree of influence over another person.

Sixteen-year-old Michael had just heard about the accidental death of a high school friend. His youth group was gathering to process the death, and he was to join them in a few minutes. But first he used the telephone to call the crisis center hot line. As he spoke on the phone, he sobbed intensely. He described himself as a deeply distraught young man, the dead youth's best friend. Michael spent most of the time crying, gesturing dramatically, and expressing deep sorrow during the youth group's meeting. Group members spent most of their time listening to him and trying to take care of his pain.

The next day something rather extraordinary happened at the funeral. Two of the deceased teen's close friends expressed their surprise at seeing Michael there. According to them, Michael and the youth had never been very close. Michael had only been posing as the dead boy's closest friend.

What was going on in this event? The death of a youth obviously disrupts an entire community of friends, whether school or church. But Michael's reaction was not born of sorrow. It was an attempt to shift attention away from the boy who had died and onto himself. He liked being the center of attention in his youth group and felt displaced when that attention shifted to another. Michael also liked to associate himself with experiences and events that made him look important. Michael badly needed to be liked, and he tried to use tears and theatrics to gain attention and affection.

The Practice of Crying

Most of us have resorted to "rehearsed crying" at one time or another. From our earliest days, we learn we can beg for attention through tears. As infants, our first "conversations" with other human beings are with a very limited vocabulary: we cooed or we cried. When our need for attention, affection, security, and safety was met promptly, we cooed and we slept peacefully. When our needs were not met promptly, we cried until somebody did something about it. We quickly learned and practiced the language of tears for immediacy and affect. Even now, as adults, we may resort to rehearsed crying from time to time if we feel all other ways to securing our needs are barred.

Some people grow up relying on rehearsed crying as a way of gaining support otherwise unavailable to them. They may have never received consistent affection and care unless they cried for it. They learned to cry in order to meet basic needs and they continue to cry whenever they feel it the most efficient means of getting what they need.

Seeking to Control

Sometimes we cry to influence someone or to control their actions. If a child cries every time a mother tries to leave the home to run errands, the mother may decide that she cannot leave the house. If we learn to cry to get what we want, we may continue crying as long as tears are successful.

Some adults cry to control their children. The aunt described earlier was trying to control her children's behavior by inducing guilt, showing them that their misbehavior "hurt" her. A teenage boy who threatens to date someone against his mother's wishes may acquiesce if mother cries every time he schedules a date. In the same manner, a college student finds herself locked into the a relationship because the coed cries each time she talks about breaking up. These and many other examples help us understand the use of tears as an attempt to control other people's actions and perceptions.

Do our tears of manipulation work? While they may well accomplish our immediate goals— we may gain attention for the moment—we may fail to see the enduring consequences, such as being labeled a manipulator.

Seeking Attention and Affection

Tears of manipulation are rarely shed because we are "bad" people. We cry such tears sometimes because we are needy. Some of us have grown up in burdened and troubled families where a parent's attention or affection were hard to get. To receive any attention or care, we had to resort to extreme behavior, such as crying. In some families, adults and children alike vie for notice and status by competing with each other in dramatic ways.

The most unfortunate side effect of tears of manipulation is that we who shed them rarely receive what we want—a clear sense that someone else cares about us. Assurance given under these circumstances is clouded by manipulation. At some level we know this and wonder if the affection is genuine.

Our tears for affection may also have a detrimental effect on our friends. If those who know us decide that our tears are contrived, they may react negatively to them and to us. People do not like to be manipulated and resent those who try. If our friends suspect our tears are affected to gain their attention, they may respond in the exact opposite way that we had hoped for. They may distance themselves from us and respond coolly to our overtures for understanding and care.

Most of us like to feel that we volunteer our interest and care toward others but bristle should anyone woo it out of us. We like to be in control of our own choices too, and like to feel that we initiate and express attention without the need for cajoling from others.

Seeking Compassion and Sympathy

We may cry tears of manipulation in order to elicit support. As a chaplain in a state prison for women, one of my responsibilities was to train chaplains and new personnel to detect rehearsed behaviors our residents used to evoke sympathy and compassion, and to gain privileges. A frequent maneuver of the residents was to rush into the chaplain's office agitated and crying, hyperventilating repeatedly, and gasping about "bad news" they had received about their families. They wanted to place unscheduled phone calls to their families. Their true motive was to evoke the chaplain's sense of compassion and sympathy to make the calls, and the sympathy of their families so family members would visit them.

We who try to "buy" compassion or sympathy from others rarely find satisfaction, even if we succeed. The reward seems hollow when we realize that compassion given under such circumstances is a direct result of our maneuvering. Sympathy means less when we suspect that we had to cry to get it. At our most human level, even the coldest of us wants to receive compassion (and any other deep feeling) from another without false inducements.

We who use tears to elicit sympathy become known as "heart tuggers." Not wanting to be deceived, our closest friends learn to approach our crying with vigilant misgiving. Instead of receiving the compassion and sympathy we seek, we evoke only caution, suspicion, emotional distance, and even dismissal.

Seeking Protection

We may use tears to communicate vulnerability to those who have power over us. Our manner can add to the message of our tears: We look scared and unprotected. Why do we send such messages? If we sense that someone might overwhelm us or intimidate us, we may resort to tears to disarm our "attacker." Some people cry in hopes of being spared from harm.

We are not suggesting that it is unimportant to feel fragile or frightened. Children subjected to the physical and emotional power of adults may have only tears for avoiding or deflecting destructive adult behaviors. Helplessness and vulnerability may be appropriately expressed in the shedding of tears.

We can, however, call up tears not so much to protect ourselves from harm as to trigger feelings of pity and generate excessive solicitude. But tears that are shed to cause people to care for us in ways we can care for ourselves are inappropriate and manipulative. Moreover, when we play on people's emotions to gain some response from them, we rarely appreciate or respect their responses. We tend to look down on people we can "work on."

The Price of Manipulative Tears

By coercing certain behaviors from others, we may rob ourselves of ongoing support. Although we may gain some vitally needed nurturing in the short run, those closest to us may withhold the long-term support and affection we seek. They may suspect our motives and protect themselves from our emotionally seductive tears by pulling away from us. The longer people are around "helpless" and weak people, the sooner they begin to understand the power we wield by looking fragile or frightened. It is not unlike the power a sick person may have over an entire family. Those who respond to our contrived tears spend time and energy helping us not cry or feel weak. But they eventually come to resent us for using them disingenuously.

People who care for us may fear our needs can never be satisfied. Professional therapists have a name for unending counseling care to people who never quit needing: compassion fatigue. But compassion fatigue is not limited to professional caregivers; family members and close friends can also succumb to caregiving burnout. And then they resent us and quit helping us.

Finally, we need to keep in mind that the people who love us and care for us have limits. We may forget that our friends have struggles and challenges of their own. Healthy relationships need balance; our friends deserve to have their needs met too.

Is there a better way to meet legitimate needs and not suffer the penalty that tears of manipulation produce? As a matter of fact, there are several ways. Let us consider them next.

Meeting Needs Without Manipulation

Those of us who have used tears to induce responses from others can find new ways to invite help without manipulation. We can learn to be clear and direct about what we legitimately need.

Perhaps the first thing we need to affirm is that attention, nurture, and sympathy—just like food, water, and shelter—are appropriate needs. We need to overcome the childhood messages that any need for attention and care is selfish. We need to remember that all of us need affection, interest, and nurture shown us—in the same measure as we need food, water, and daily rest. Problems arrive only when we ask for excessive amounts. The few people who need help setting boundaries on their needs are those who have neglected them to the point of imbalance.

Asking for Affection and Attention

Asking for things we need may seem awkward to us at first. We are accustomed to waiting and hoping that people around us will guess what we need or be able to somehow pick up on our indirect hints. Such an approach is very ineffective. A more appropriate and effective approach to getting our significant needs met is to express them to others and then invite them to respond.

Betty grew up in a family that expressed affection physically. She married Ralph, one of six children in a family that was very verbal, but not physical, about expressing love. After spending the first four months of her marriage feeling that Ralph had quit loving her, Betty talked with a counselor. She complained that Ralph never hugged her when they greeted each other at the beginning and end of the day. She cried over his apparent indifference, but her tears only seemed to distance him.

As she explored the issue with her counselor, Betty discovered that her internal confirmation of being loved by her parents was their long, comforting hugs as she left for the day and returned in the evening. Then it dawned on her that Ralph's parents rarely showed affection to each other in her presence. When the counselor suggested to Betty that she ask for a hug when she wanted one, she resisted the idea as contrived. But Betty, hungry as she was to receive affection from her husband, decided to ask. Ralph was eager to oblige and responded with increased passion as the months passed. He was surprised that such a simple gesture meant so much to his wife and reduced her tears.

We are not suggesting that Betty's tears were inappropriate. Our tears can be genuine expressions of deeply-felt needs. Betty felt neglected and unloved; but she needed to explain her needs to Ralph so that he could respond to them. To Ralph, Betty's initial tears came without any explanation and appeared to be rehearsed behavior designed to make him feel guilty. What Betty learned to do was to ask for what she needed from a caring husband who had not learned a key term in Betty's "language" of affection and love—the hug.

If we live far away from nurturing family members, or if we belong to a dysfunctional family that cannot respond to our needs for support, we need to look to our immediate communities for persons who can and will meet some of these needs appropriately. In each of the communities where I have lived, I have selected a few relationships that I can trust, inviting those I can trust to a "covenant of nurture" with me. In that commitment, we each pledge to meet regularly (every two weeks), keep up with each others' concerns, ask for nurture, and be safe and reliable friends. Our covenants usually last six to eight months; although, most of the participants opt to stay in longer. We thus create for ourselves a network nurturing of persons.

Asking for Support

Sometimes we feel isolated and alone, and we want our loved ones to give us support. Unfortunately, we often want them to guess what we need. But we are far more likely to receive support when we simply say what we need.

Jim came home distressed at the additional amount of work he had been assigned by his boss. He felt his office was already short-handed and that he was being asked to do a greater amount of work with the newly-assigned projects. He wanted his wife to notice his distress and ask about it, but when she didn't, he went upstairs to pout over being "neglected." Meanwhile, his wife felt that Jim had neglected her by going upstairs without an explanation or noticing the dinner she had prepared. She put the food away with tears in her eyes. When Jim asked her what she was crying about, she said it was nothing.

Jim would have had a better chance of getting the support he sought by telling his wife how he felt used and neglected at work and that he needed her to listen to him talk about it. She, too, would probably have gained support by reminding her husband that she was tired and needed to hear more supportive comments about her efforts to provide the evening meal.

Asking for Protection

There are times in life when we feel more vulnerable than usual. Sometimes we seek protection, as mentioned, by shedding tears. We have every right to seek protection when we feel fragile. The irony of manipulative tears, however, is that such displays of vulnerability in childhood often attracted abusive relationships that took advantage of our fragile condition.

Mary Beth was in her fourth month of divorce from a severely abusive husband. I had listened to her sorrow and her pain sometimes twice a week during that difficult first month in which she had isolated herself from family and friends and had become suicidal. She had relied on phone calls and hospital visits from me when she felt hopeless. Now she was better, but she faced another danger.

"I need to make some changes for my own sake," she told me. "I've appreciated your care and constant support these past few months, and I feel stronger—and more hopeful. Now I need your help finding a counselor I can trust—because I shouldn't see you anymore." Her eyes filled with tears, but she shook them away and continued: "You're too kind for me right now, Dan . . . I've grown accustomed to your gentle nature, and I feel very vulnerable around you. I need to leave you so that I can regain my balance and so that I don't try to woo you with my pain. I'd love to try, but I don't want to misuse you—or myself. I'm stronger and stable, so this is a good time to make a shift. I'm having trouble seeing you as my counselor. I'm beginning to dream about you, so I need some space from you. I hope you understand."

And I did understand. Mary Beth needed my help maintaining a distance. She needed to protect herself—and me—from her vulnerable condition. She chose to trust me with her vulnerability without using her tears to play on my emotions. She was inviting me to help her find safety and space by telling me what she needed in order to preserve her dignity and self-respect.

Not all of us can be as clear as Mary Beth was about her needs. We can, however, declare our vulnerability in a few relationships where trust is established. We can pay attention to inner promptings that alert us to our susceptibility to hurt, and ask people we trust to covenant with us to protect us. Mary Beth was asking me to respect her needs for safety—and to help her secure protection for herself.

When we are at risk, tears are normal and expected. Though our tears in such circumstances may also be a cry for compassion and safety, we learn that God has never promised to protect us from all danger in these valleys, but has promised to walk with us through the risks (Psalm 23). Tears of manipulation that seek rescue from danger are wishful tears that cry out for safety in a careless world. As long as we understand that God cannot promise us unconditional protection, we have every right to cry and to seek protection.

Such tears give birth to a strength that nurtures us through the unavoidable wounds of life. Even though God cannot be manipulated, our cries are heard. Our pleas for protection and safety are heard even as Jesus' cries from the cross were heard in the silence of that awful morning. And though we are not protected from all the harm in this world—that still not subject to God's rule—we have the promise in the Book of Revelation that one day, in a world where God rules without interruption, there will be safety beyond tears.

Beyond Manipulation: The Challenge

Old patterns do not change overnight. We manipulate primarily because we have learned not to trust relationships. Trusting other people is a risk; we will need patience to experiment with trusting. Cautious, careful attempts will reward us with reassurance that we can be honest with others and trust them with our needs. Genuine relationships require trust, however, and we are the ones most to gain from the challenge of learning how to relate to others without deceit and manipulation.

Unless we choose to act openly and honestly in handling our relationships, we will continue to flirt with the need to influence others by deceit. Our openness and trust with others, however, can provide us a new freedom—freedom from coercion or deceit.

To break free of manipulation, we must first choose to practice an honest and straightforward way of sharing our needs. Then, and only then, will we experience the satisfaction of being known and valued for who we are, and of getting our need for attention, affection, compassion, and support met without an angle.

Chapter 10

―――――――◆――――――――

Tears of Pain

I held my wounded body straight—and walked ahead;
I held my head up high, to hide my wounded soul.
I held my pain inside, afraid to cry—
and show my wound again, and slowly die.

SOMETIMES WE CRY BECAUSE WE HURT. The infant, feeling the pangs of hunger in his stomach, cries over his discomfort. The child, falling as she runs down the sidewalk, cries over her hurting knee. The teenager, rejected by a person she likes, cries over the hurt feelings. The young adult, clutching a letter of rejection from his college of choice, cries over the loss of a dream. The tears of pain commingle with our tears of failure, fatigue, and frustration.

There are several shapes to pain and, therefore, several shapes to tears of pain. We cry when we hurt physically, emotionally, or spiritually. Tears are an immediate response to injury and, though they cannot heal our wounds, they give voice to our distress and alert our friends to our suffering.

He tries so hard to be tough, to fight back. He has a reputation as a fighter. But the weeks, the months—yes, the lifetime—of racism seemed too large a burden to bear. His jaw quivered as he fought back the pain—but to no avail. Tears squeezed out the corners of his dark eyes and slid freely down his cheeks. He sobbed in my arms. I wept with him, feeling for once, the depth of his hurt. Pain brought by a difference he can't—he shouldn't want to—change. His tears washed away the film that had distorted my white perspective of the world.

Sometimes we want to hide our tears of pain. Infants are born with an understanding that expressing pain is normal. But boys in our culture are regularly taught that "big boys don't cry" because crying is a sign of weakness. Consequently, some of us learn in childhood to feel ashamed of showing any signs of pain, as if we should be embarrassed for hurting.

Unless we learn differently, we emerge as adults who feel embarrassed about expressing pain. Counselors continually report how embarrassed their patients feel when a relationship dissolves, and they express their pain with tears. We regularly have to remind people that God made us for bonding, trusting, and connecting in relationships, and that we never need to feel embarrassed for loving—or hurting. Actually, our tears of pain are an eloquent testimony of our capacity to bond and care as God intended. Such tears are a symbol of emotional maturity.

Tears are one of our most therapeutic ways of expressing pain. With our tears we say that we have been wounded—sometimes physically, sometimes emotionally, sometimes spiritually. What does pain do to us, and what can we learn from our tears of pain?

Pain: Physical, Emotional, Spiritual

From time to time we read about the tragic experience of a child born without the nerve neurons that register physical pain and send that message to the brain. At first glance, some folks think of such a condition as a blessing. (They can do anything and never feel pain!) But a second look provides a far more alarming and dangerous picture: people who cannot register pain can injure themselves seriously and not know it. Our pain nerve network is a security system designed to alert the brain that a specific part of the body is experiencing injury and needs attention.

Tears are a natural response to pain. The child who bumps her head on the furniture cries tears of pain. The hospitalized patient losing the effects of an anesthetic after surgery, cries tears of pain. The expectant mother cries tears of pain while giving birth to her child. Some of us must manage the uncomfortable throbbing of joints and muscles in a body hampered by arthritis. To declare our wounds and express distress, we cry tears of pain.

Tears of pain come when we face the stress of terminal illness. The discovery of a malignancy or another life-threatening disease almost immediately humbles us emotionally. The shock of such news brings on natural grief. As the disease progresses and our physical pain increases, we cry because of the physical and emotional suffering we endure. Folks who don't understand the raw reality of such pain cannot understand our need to weep. Friends who try to console us by trying to stop our tears fail to understand their function in releasing our pain. Perhaps we ourselves fail to understand the healing value of our tears.

Pain is not just a physical experience. The despairing partner in a marriage, aware that there is no hope for a reconciliation with a spouse; the driver of a car involved in an accident fatal to his passengers; the teenage mother, surrendering her newborn child for adoption—all feel the agony of emotional pain.

Pain can also have spiritual dimensions. Some of us experience alienation from a childhood faith that was inadequate during traumatic events in our life. The agony that some of us suffer when we encounter flat seasons in our spiritual growth is the cause of much "spiritual trauma." The pain of betraying one's own moral or ethical code can also be severe.

In his book, *Tears, Idle Tears*, biochemist William H. Frey tells us that our tears serve as carriers of stress-filled body chemicals that our eyes discharge from our bodies to relieve us. His ongoing research involves reports from stressed people who claim to feel better after crying and sweating. It seems that the discharge of toxic material from our bodies may restore a chemical balance to us when we are stressed or depressed. Our tears of pain, then, are intentional instruments of healing.

While tears still hold some mystery for us, we continue to discover their therapeutic function in the experience of pain. Those of us who cry when suffering may experience the first elements of comfort, healing, and recovery. Certainly paying attention to our tears will help all of us better understand how to care for ourselves when we hurt.

What We Need When We Hurt

Those of us who live in the shadow of constant physical pain need understanding of our tears. They are our poured out to give voice to our distress, not as an attempt to cause a loved one to hurt with us.

> Why is my pain unending
> and my wound grievous and incurable?
> Will you be to me like a deceptive brook,
> like a spring that fails? (Jeremiah 15:18)

We who suffer also need patience matched with understanding when we live with the constancy of our suffering. We need patience because we must live with the recurring ebb and flow of our condition. We cannot be rushed through our pain. We need those who listen to us not to grow weary listening to our pain as we travel through it. Living with it requires patience, and those who share our suffering as companions to our lamentations gift us when they show patience.

The word in the New Testament that we translate as "long-suffering" in the King James Version of the Bible means an "enduring patience that waits long enough to conquer." Our friends bless us when they can endure the wait we endure.

In the midst of our suffering, loved ones can further support us by simply remaining with us through some of the hurt. Jesus Christ asked three of his disciples to remain nearby while he cried and prayed in pain. He was asking for what all of us need: companionship in our suffering. Our need is not for people who will suffer while we do. We seek a few friends who choose to remain beside us during our pain because they are willing to be present while we hurt.

The sustaining power of companionship has always made pain more bearable. We are strengthened by loved ones who "bear us up" in our tears. Crying produces a bond that sustains us in our weakest moments. Our weakness is made strong when we cry with those who care for us. The apostle Paul challenged the Galatians to such care when he referred to the power that a community of faith provides the burdened by their willing presence: "Bear one another's burdens."

What we need to know (and need others to know) is that the tears we shed during suffering are allies in our survival. Contrary to the common view that they may hinder us, our tears help us expel our pain and dispose of toxic stress.

Emotional Pain

We also shed tears for suffering that has no physical cause. Emotional pain is as draining as physical pain. The tears we shed are again, as in physical suffering, an attempt to restore balance within us.

In the popular novel *The Prince of Tides*, author Pat Conroy details the story of a man who carries the dark secrets of a family tragedy when he and his siblings were children. As a counselor gains his trust, he slowly unwraps the emotionally charged episode of a break-in in which his mother, his sister, and he are each raped. The struggling boy, trying to protect his family from the attackers, turns upon his assailants and kills one of them. As man and therapist gingerly uncover the secret the former has been hiding, the man breaks down in convulsive tears. There, in the relived suffering of that awful day, the boy inside the man expresses his stored emotional pain.

Emotional suffering comes in several forms. The woman who cannot give birth; the mother whose dreams for her child are shattered by the young woman's elopement; the son who wants to be blessed by a father who prefers his brother—all cry tears of rejection and pain.

Many of us carry the silent pain of bitter disappointments. The personal ridicule, the rejection, the neglect, and the emotional injury in our primary relationships travel with us through a lifetime of tears. For example, we may be the unblessed child in a family of celebrated children. The tears we shed at first were deep inside, but eventually seeped into the public eye. Or we might be the loyal employee who has consistently worked hard and has been passed over for promotion. Or we might shed tears over potential never realized. We review choices we made along our journeys, and weep over experiences not available or not tried; for talents not developed, goals not achieved, and aspirations not seriously entertained.

Not only do we hurt for ourselves, but for others, too. We weep for family members whose burden or choice has made life unpleasant. We cry for friends who never experience the intimacy they deserve because they cannot, or will not, risk emotional openness in a relationship. We shed tears of distress for friends who fail to reach their potential, dreams, or their promise.

What We Need Emotionally

Tears of pain bring us to moments when prayer can mean a lot. In the discovering our helplessness, we turn to a power greater than our own. Our prayers help us face our limitations and invite the power and presence of God to the threshold of our injuries.

We pray not to manipulate life or people, but to invoke God's presence that we believe is good and hopeful in the face of our limited resources. We pray for God's perspective, because God can give us a sense of proportion in our pain. Emotional pain can be so intense that we lose sight of the degree of our wounds. We pray for God's presence to provide us with insight— beyond our capacities. We ask for the comfort and healing of a God who can respond to us and intervene by giving us access to a power that helps us through our pain.

Our first request of God in our pain is that God's presence may assuage our suffering and give us strength to endure the journey our pain may require. We also pray for courage not to be defeated in our agony, for patience to overcome our pain, and for faith that we can heal. We pray for insight and discernment, such that even the pain we endure may provide us with a hidden blessing of newfound strength, character, or steadfastness—as only God can help us find. As Paul explained to the Roman Christians, we learn that suffering can produce endurance, endurance can produce character, and character can produce hope.

We may also pray for those who hurt us, that they may see and understand the harm they have caused. We pray that they may understand the truth shared for their good, and that they may find relief from pressures that bind them and cause them to act in destructive ways. In addition, we can ask God to restore them to postures that will save them or heal them. Because we hurt, we pray for insight into the actions of others, so that we may not be deprived of the release of forgiving them. We ask God for understanding where possible. We also ask for faith and patience when understanding is absent—and when we must wait.

Spiritual Pain

Personal pain is an inclusive human struggle and includes a spiritual dimension. All of us wrestle at one time or other with experiences and beliefs that evoke a "suffering of the spirit." Some experiences cause us a sickness of the soul. There are moments when we feel divided and disturbed from within; at other times, we feel the agony of being at odds with creation and the God who created. Such times have been called the "winter of the soul."

I listened as the missionary to Bangladesh described the ebbing sea that surrendered its dead in the aftermath of a typhoon that took the coast by surprise:

> Most of the dead were the vulnerable poor who had no
> place to live, and "squatted" on the edge of the Indian
> Ocean in shacks off the land. They had no place to run
> when the waters came; now, buried by the hundreds in a

watery grave, they had resurfaced as limp bodies floating in
a fickle sea. How unfair! How merciless is nature!
Deprived first of comfort, then of home, and now of life
itself—these innocent victims of nature toss in quiet waters
as worthless leftovers of a capricious providence. . . . My
stomach cramped in pain.

Allied soldiers freeing Jewish prisoners of war in Germany in
1945 experienced a similar inward pain. Sometimes we struggle
with the injustices of life and identify with the suffering of the
bystander. Pain permeates everything we believe in and grieves
us deeply. The agony of internalizing someone else's undeserved
suffering so that we feel it ourselves is called moral or spiritual
pain.

Some of us experience another form of spiritual suffering
when our faith system is bankrupt and we live in the winter sea-
son of the soul. Facing doubt and disengagement for the first
time, we become discouraged and depressed. In the throes of
what we have often called the absence of God, most of us feel
deceived or abandoned. For some of us the discouragement
becomes heavy enough that we cry. Encountering the possibility
of a faithless future, we cry from anticipation of life without purpose—and without God.

Wade Clark Roof is one of several sociologists who has tried
to identify this spiritual pain specifically in the so-called "baby
boom" generation. Affluent and successful adults in the latter
part of this century are struggling with an inner emptiness that
has caused us to search for meaning and value beyond financial stability and status. This spiritual thirst signals a strong
quest for purposes and beliefs to fill the void that has left many
in spiritual pain.

Those of us who have drawn strength and purpose from
beliefs and values that have shaped our spiritual journey find any
spiritual desert uncomfortable. The emergence of a new truth
that shatters previously unchallenged beliefs can drive us into
uncharted and unsafe ground. What we knew and staked our life
on most of the time may suddenly come under intense judgment.

We stagger spiritually with issues that question our foundations. With the psalmist of old, we are bewildered by events that force us to question whether what we do has any meaning—and whether God can be found at work in our pain.

There is also a time when we must own our spiritual values. The movement from borrowed beliefs to personal affirmations can be a treacherous, painful ground. Living between what we have always heard and what we now personally affirm causes anxiety. The silence and the waiting cause us pain; our questions seemed hurled out at no one, and the answers received seem inadequate. The valley of spiritual self-discovery involves suffering. Many a soul has cried through the night seeking a spiritual dawn.

What do we need to know in our spiritual distress? First of all, we must know that many others have experienced the same suffering and turmoil. We need to remember that they also survived: Jacob in Haran, Moses in Midian, Elijah in the wilderness, Hezekiah in Judah, Peter in Caesarea, Paul in Asia. We can also take courage that in each case these often weak human beings emerged stronger in the broken places.

We who cry tears of spiritual pain need to learn the persistence of Jacob and Job. Jacob wrestled with his Maker until he secured a blessing (after trying so hard to steal it years before!). Job argued with his Creator until he walked through many losses to the other side. We, too, must sometimes strive with God. We may need to wrestle with God (and ourselves) until the ornaments of our beliefs become the garments of our faith.

Author Gore Vidal, in an interview on a television program years ago, said that our American society idolizes the "superficial and the immediate." Both temptations are instructive to any of us who struggle with spiritual pain. Our path to healing in spiritual suffering involves both a capacity to use our waiting creatively and a determination to embrace the deeper issues and answers in life.

Conquering Our Pain

One of the realities of life is that sometimes pain does not go away. But even when healing is not possible, we can learn to find courage, endurance, and hope. We've mentioned elsewhere how the apostle Paul struggled with the inevitability of physical pain. A minister friend served a congregation in Waco, Texas for over thirty-five years as pastor, living the last twelve years of his ministry in a wheelchair, drawn up by the torturing disease of muscular dystrophy. He died in his early fifties, celebrated by a church and community that filled a university chapel to affirm his life and faith.

How do we muster the will to go on in the midst of continuous pain? Wayne E. Oates, a mentor and colleague who has inspired many ministers and teachers in America, has lived with a searing, nagging back condition for more than thirty years. Despite several surgeries, he is still often bedridden. Nevertheless, Oates has continued to write, lecture, and speak. With his son, a medical specialist in Kentucky, Oates co-authored a book on pain, its eroding effects, and the redemptive outlook of a conquering spirit.

What makes it possible for us to conquer emotional pain? Martin Seligman and Lillian Rubin, in separate studies of children deprived and abused in childhood, have celebrated the capacity of the human spirit to conquer suffering and take charge of life. Research continues to suggest that our body releases positive or negative chemicals in our blood stream during periods of stress and disease. How we see life and how we respond to difficulty apparently has a lot to do with our capacity to survive and to maintain hope during trauma. Tears of pain provide us with a crossroads between purpose and defeat in our travel. How we choose to live during our suffering is crucial to the hope we may have in our journey through tomorrow's pain.

The Greek word for patience (makrothumia) that Paul uses in Galatians is most properly translated as "a conquering endurance." According to the apostle, evidence of the Holy Spirit's presence in the life of a believer was the development of an attitude that outlasted and outlived any difficulty. Christians, Paul declared, had available to them a presence that sustained them through all adversities, and a power that enabled them to conquer in spite of any injury. Such strength brought courage to the persecuted believer, and confidence to the wounded soul.

We can experience this empowerment in our own lives by asking God to inhabit our mind and heart. The strength to conquer is born within us by a spirit greater than ours who breathes life, strength, and hope into our soul. We must also be willing to cooperate with the spirit's power within us by nurturing a conquering attitude over our pain ourselves. By choosing to believe that God can give us strength to overcome physical, emotional, or spiritual adversities, we prepare our own spirit to receive the conquering power of God's presence.

Sir Winston Churchill, whose voice galvanized Great Britain during the darkest days of the Second World War, delivered his former high school's shortest commencement speech when he stood up, stared intensely into the students' faces, and shouted: "Never—never—never—never—never—give up!" The great British motivator, aware of his own frailties early in his career, learned to trust God for endurance when his country faced its worst suffering.

Creative waiting involves a willingness to patiently explore the road of personal discovery even in our pain. Whether our tears are over physical, emotional, or spiritual wounds, we can conquer our suffering by learning to faithfully endure—and by trusting a God who will grace us with strength for every trial we face.

In the meantime, we who cry tears of pain can conquer our aching through patient labor. If we refuse to settle for quick answers in our journey of faith, our search will reward us with worthwhile strong values and beliefs. If we avoid the superficial and the simple answers in our quest for inner peace, we will eventually discover the "pearl of great price," the deepest and most rewarding realities and purposes. Then, and possibly only then, will our tears of pain disappear. In their place will be values and purposes that will bring us fulfillment and excitement about living. We shall thank our tears for carrying away the tension of our pain, and ushering us to a new dimension of faith: the experience of conquering our pain and learning from it. Even joy and peace may follow.

Chapter 11

———————— •—•—• ————————

Tears of Sorrow

And have I lost before — and know not grief, you ask?
And have I lived, and never lost?
And have I loved, and never grieved?
And have I, then, not truly lived?

I HEARD THE NEWS AS I WALKED IN THE OFFICE: Marge Simpson's husband, a young military helicopter pilot, only three weeks overseas, had been killed in action. The air force representative had just left her parents' house, where Marge and her two-year-old son had settled to wait out her husband's term of service.

I had known Marge only for a short while, since she had returned to our area. Her parents were very active in our church and eager to provide her stability during the long wait for her husband's return. I had also met Jim, her husband, during a few quick visits. I remember Marge's anxiety as he prepared to leave for his thirteen-month assignment.

I was filled with dread and sorrow as I called, but they needed care, and I was one of their pastors. When her father answered the phone, I told him how stunned I was about the horrible news. Then Marge was on the phone, crying instantly.

"Where was your God when my husband needed him? What am I going to do? I just want to die!"

"Marge, may I come over for a few minutes?" I asked, knowing how agitated she was, and guessing how anxious her parents were about her care.

"What good would that do? Is that going to bring him back? Are you going to promise me that everything is going to be all right? I want my husband back! Can you do that? "

"I want to come over for a few minutes," I said. "Unless you tell me that you'd rather I not come now, I'm about to drive over there. . . ." After a moment, Marge's father got on the phone and said it would be all right if I went over.

John met me at the door, his face solemn and ashen. He took me directly into the living room, where his daughter was sitting, and left me to visit with Marge. Her fists were clenched, her eyes worn from crying, her face flushed; used tissues were piled up next to her. She glared at me.

"What am going to tell my child?" she asked, her eyes filled with tears. "What kind of God would do this to me? Don't come in here and tell me that God has a reason for this! I'm warning you, I don't want to hear any stupid God-explanations right now!"

I listened to her pour out her grief. She took turns crying and talking. Sometimes she yelled at me, or at God, as she juggled the immeasurable pain inside her. After about half an hour, she was exhausted.

"I want to be of help, Marge, without getting in the way. I'm so sorry . . . and I can't imagine your pain and anger. Please let me know when you want me to talk, to listen, to leave, to wait, or help with decisions you may have to make. . . . I know you're tired. I hope you can rest some. . . . Shall we screen your visits and your calls—so that you can decide if you're up to talking with people? Call me—or have your family call—if you would care to talk."

She nodded a moment and softly thanked me for coming by. I thanked her for letting me stop by and trusting me with her pain. Then I sat there for a few more minutes, to give her a chance to say more if she wanted to. She was calmer now and breathing more slowly.

I suggested to John and Lois that Marge be encouraged to rest. I explained that she would sometimes want privacy, and sometimes would not want to be alone. I said they were free to call me or ask that I come by. I mentioned that if their daughter found resting difficult, they might consider some prescription medication. I reminded them that they needed rest, too, and that rest would help them care for Marge.

Then I poked my head into the room where Marge was sitting, and knowing her parents could hear me, too, I said, "I'm asking your folks to protect you by calling me or a paramedic, or to take you to the hospital if they fear for your safety. I'm encouraging them to get you help if you ever sound like you want to hurt yourself, because your life is important to us. I hope you tell them clearly if you need help taking care of yourself. If they are in doubt, know to call someone who can help them decide. We want you around, and taken care of. Do you understand what I'm trying to say, Marge? I don't want them wondering if you are going to hurt yourself, or kill yourself, so I hope you can ask for help when you're hurting badly." I waited a moment, and she nodded.

I suggested to John and Lois that Marge not be left completely alone for the next few days—her pain and anger made her more vulnerable than usual. Then I called the church office in their hearing, and suggested that the deacon ministry network help with food and other needs. We made a list of close friends who Marge might welcome for brief, announced visits during the next few days. They could provide daily doses of the support and encouragement Marge needed.

Caring for Marge would involve a great deal. How do we survive when we experience such a traumatic loss? Marge's bitter tears were a natural response to the unfair loss of a loved one and to the helplessness we face with the dreaded finality of death. Marge's rage and agony needed to be heard—not argued or evaluated. The intensity of her feelings was a measure of her love and loss.

To appreciate the power of sorrow, we may need to remember that we care and love because God made us to bond, and that we value companionship because God does. Such linkage makes losing someone a deeply painful event. To care is to value, to lose is to hurt, with no control over the loss.

Over the years, caregivers have identified a particular set of responses to the loss of a loved one. Shock, numbness, depression, bursts of stabbing pain, selective memory, anger, guilt, and paralyzing moods are some of our normal reactions. The sudden, tragic death of a person dear to us can evoke even stronger reactions.

The First Painful Questions

Most of us can be overwhelmed when faced with the unexpected. Death is a stunning reality. The sudden awareness that we have been permanently robbed of a loved one is hard to absorb. Shock and numbness are protective first responses to an anguish that might otherwise be unbearable. The pain of loss and our helplessness to reverse it are deeply distressing realities. We stare in disbelief and confusion in the face of death's permanence and the mystery of tragic events. Anger, frustration, bitterness, and resentment usually follow.

Feeling that we have lost control over life and happiness, we usually struggle with powerlessness. In our pain, we look for a cause, an explanation, or some source of comfort or control. Most of us who grow up with any religious instruction look for a power beyond our own that we may somehow summon to take charge. At the same time that we call on God, we wonder where God is and whether God cares about us when we suffer and lose. We want God (or someone) to do something about our seemingly unbearable misery. If God is good, why did this happen? If God is in charge, why won't God change it? If God cares, why do we feel abandoned?

All of us experience sorrow. Recently my wife and I attended a play in which three different family clusters were struggling to accept the reality of a terminal illness in the family. After the play, actors and audience gathered to process the message of the drama. Someone in the audience asked if the characters in the play would have responded differently to the reality of loss if they had been Christians. I suggested that I had not assumed that they weren't believers, as everyone suffers loss. Christ felt deep sorrow at the death of Lazarus. While he strained to accept death, Christ also grieved in Gethsemane, because he hated the loss of his own life and friend.

Some religious traditions (and early biblical stories) interpreted all events as caused by God. Ancient Jews attributed all happenings to God because they knew no other explanation for natural disasters and human crises. Later, in the Scriptures, the keen observer concluded that if human beings were given freedom to do as they pleased, then not all actions could be blamed on God. Although it is still common today to hear popular religious leaders speak of every death as "God's will," most of us understand that God is not responsible for all death and loss. In an imperfect world where accident, evil, and human choice are at work, God hurts with us in the sorrows of loss.

In our society, most of us think little about death or tragedy unless it strikes someone we love. Faced with our own sorrow, we experience truth that we are not in control of everything. We look for someone who is in charge to regain control ourselves.

Is there a purpose to our tragic loss? Those of us who shed the tears of sorrow also contend with the popular notion that "there must be a purpose" to every event. Joy, death, or tragedy are all said to have a reason. We are usually asked to find this hidden reason ourselves. Anxious friends often provide us such explanations in hope of comforting us. Quite often it is they who seek some comfort by explaining mysteries they cannot understand. Rather than comfort us, such comments may convey the notion of a whimsical God who creates tragedy and death to "teach us a lesson."

We have every right to be angry about such careless views of God's activity in our misfortunes. Behind such misconceptions is the idea that God must cause everything; and, because God cannot possibly "do wrong," there must be some hidden purpose to be discerned in every event. Already feeling cheated by death, we do not need to hear that we must search through the debris of our loss to find a hidden, divine intent.

It is one thing to affirm that God can take any tragic event and make some good of it (even though no one finds such reminders comforting in the throes of a loss); it is quite another thing to blame God for an evil occurrence and to require that burdened people "discover" God's hidden reason for a catastrophe.

Such wounds are further aggravated by comments such as "God should never be questioned." In our sadness we need to be assured that God will listen to anything we have to say and that we may question God as much as the psalmists did. We need to know that our questions are part of our faith—not cynical disbelief. People who tell us not to question God are trying to control our anxiety and their own; we feel vulnerable when we have no ready answers for misfortune. Unfortunately, many people have learned such religious "catch phrases" in the local church. Sorrow-stricken people aren't helped by such remarks; we are usually stifled, angered, or confused by them.

When we have suffered a loss, we need to know that someone understands the depth of our anguish. We feel quite helpless in knowing where to take our complaint. Like the psalmist, we sometimes need to rail at God because we care, and because we hope God cares—enough to listen to our agony. We need to be reassured that God understands the sadness behind our complaint, and will not stifle or dismiss our feelings. We need to know that we do not have to edit our anger in order to "manage" a temperamental deity. We need the assurance that God can manage our loss and frustration.

Our tears of sorrow are released in bitterness, frustration, and sadness. We are not helped through such valleys of tears unless these feelings are received, acknowledged, and validated.

Expressing the Sorrow of Loss

As chaplain to a women's prison in Kentucky several years ago, one of my responsibilities was to deliver important family news to the residents. On one occasion, I had been counseling a woman who had almost committed suicide when her husband rejected her. After several months of recovery, she was stable.

She developed a new sense of hope when her husband decided to try the marriage again. He was on his way to a third visit with her at the prison, two weeks before her parole, when he was killed in an automobile accident.

The inmate was so traumatized that only way she felt she could express her sorrow was to hurt herself. She had to be restrained. She needed sedation to calm down and eventually sleep.

Medical experts remind us that the intensity generated by anger actually produces chemical and physiological changes in our body. Anger triggers the release of the hormones adrenaline and cortisol into the bloodstream, which mobilize the body by increasing the heart rate and blood pressure, and stimulate fat cells to empty into the bloodstream to provide a quick source of energy. Under extended pressure, these hormones also seem to suppress the immune system, making the angry person more susceptible to illness.

That is why medical help is desirable for people struggling with heavy bouts of anger and distress. Some people require medication to help them through the peak feelings. Some people need no medication. In either case, it is essential to monitor our capacity to contain our turmoil. One of the first gifts people can offer us as we cry tears of sorrow is to receive us in our agony.

Accepting the Initial Agony of Sorrow

People help us most who "receive" our agony by listening with care to our anguish. We need friends who allow us to cry out in our helplessness, and who allow us to give voice to our anger at being robbed of love. When we feel the overwhelming anguish of loss, we need someone who understands our need to voice shock, numbness, anger, and many other early signals of loss. To stifle our feelings is to delay our healing. Tears of sorrow are often our first visible expression of grief. The cry of the lover who has lost a loved one needs to be uttered:

> A voice is heard in Ramah, mourning and great weep-
> ing, Rachel weeping for her children and refusing to be
> comforted, because her children are no more
> (Jeremiah 31:15).

As Israel wept the loss of Rachel (and Rachel weeps for
her children separated from her), we also express our sorrows
in the release of tears. The apostle Paul, in his letter to believers in Rome, explained that there are times in our life when
we have no words to explain our condition, and the Spirit of
God intercedes for us with sighs too deep for words. The
Bible has an entire volume dedicated to the expression of sorrow over personal loss, the death of a city, a nation, a people:
the Book of Lamentations. Giving voice and focus to our
agony channels our feelings like a river bed receives and con-
tains a river. The flow of our agony seeks a way out so that it
will not wreak havoc on the inside. Headaches, digestive
pains, and numerous other physical ailments may be internal
responses to bottled up grief.

Some people become anxious when we cry out, because
they feel helpless themselves to "fix" us. But those who understand the importance of lamentation know, with the prophet Isa-
iah, that to "bear each other's grief and carry each other's sorrows" means to enable the healing to take place.

Acknowledging the Power of Loss and Bitterness

Death and the first reality of separation from love provide us an
opportunity to acknowledge the depth of our love. The strength
of our sorrow is the measure of our loss; we affirm with our tears
and our agony the power of a relationship dear to us.

Grieving the loss of a loved one often means coming to terms
with the finality of death. We realize that we can no longer speak
to the deceased, touch her, or express our love to her in this life.
Regrets and hopes come crashing in as we review the moment
and accept the reality that our time with the person has ended in
this physical world.

One of the more difficult tasks we face is dealing with our bitterness. Loss is a bitter reality. The sense of being cheated or robbed of an important relationship is profound. Part of grieving is allowing the bitterness to run its course.

Bitterness, like anger, has little to do with faith. The profound anguish of loss has a ragged edge, and it is natural to need both distance from God and closeness to God. Reluctantly, we take turns embracing the finality of separation and grasping at the fantasy that we may just be having a bad dream. We hope someone will have pity on us and magically return our loved ones.

Sorrow Over Many "Deaths"

We all experience many kinds of "death" during our lifetimes: a broken relationship, a divorce, a friendship ended, a vocation concluded, a home we must leave. All too rarely do we appreciate the importance of "grief work" during such times.

When a relationship we value is broken, we travel through some very recognizable stages of disengagement. Ministers and other caregivers are familiar with the traumatic journey of grief work. The following are descriptions of some of the parts we usually experience:

Shock. We are stunned by the unexpected news that a relationship is over and respond in a dazed, detached manner; we are out of touch with our feelings and act "frozen" and distant. Our thoughts and emotions seem far away; there are no tears in our eyes.

Numbness. We experience a lack of sensation and an absence of affect. Numbed by the news of a broken relationship, we stand between reality and unreality and have little or no awareness of feeling. It is as if an anesthetic had been administered to our bodies. Even though we can talk and go through motions, we are unable to respond with feeling. Tears are still absent.

Release of Emotions. Following initial moments (or days) of shock and numbness, we feel pain, we begin to cry, and we become conscious of our deep anguish. Our tears are heavy. It is not unusual to cry for long periods of time and wonder if we will ever quit crying. At times, we cry ourselves into exhaustion. Tears and feelings erupt in sudden, intense bursts. We are in touch with our pain, and the impact of our sorrow is deep. We fear losing control.

Depression. Bouts of depression alternate with moments of quiet and calm; unexpected mood shifts make us wonder if we'll ever feel better and whether life is worth living. All excitement and joy are gone; life seems empty, joyless. We want to retreat from view, hide from others, and quit our schedules and routines. Tears come and go.

Anger. We begin to review the broken relationship and get angry with ourselves for making any mistakes we feel contributed to the interruption of the bond. We also get angry with ourselves for allowing ourselves to get so emotionally involved with another person. When we are not angry with ourselves, we are angry with the person who left for rejecting us or for abandoning the relationship. We feel angry with the partner also if we conclude that we were used or deceived in the relationship. If tears fall, they are the tears of anger.

Guilt. Guilt alternates with anger as we blame ourselves for the failure of the relationship or take responsibility for creating stress and discomfort in the relationship and precipitating its demise. We also struggle with boundaries we feel we did not honor in the relationship and behaviors we feel were contrary to our values—or at least inconsistent with the level of commitment we thought we had prior to the breakup.

Stabbing memories. Having recovered enough balance in our own life to maintain a routine, we are troubled by sudden reminders of the loved one, or memories that revive our sorrow. Other emotions can quickly change from peace and contentment to insecurity, depression, and tears.

Selective reflection. We review the relationship in a skewed and irrational way, selecting memories that idealize (or vilify) our partners. We remember our participation in the relationship unrealistically, telling ourselves that we either did everything right or everything wrong. Few tears now flow.

Return to routine. We command ourselves to return to the schedules and requirements of living. There is no joy in our work, and we feel vulnerable and foolish for having loved and lost. Our self-esteem is low, and we function day-to-day, exhausted by the amount of energy expended in maintenance and survival. We feel very lonely, unlovable, and in need of care. We doubt ourselves and wonder if we can ever regain our capacity to love or trust another relationship. Tears are rare.

Gradual recovery of joy. Our banal routines are interrupted by moments of laughter and joy. We notice more time between our sad moments and bouts of depression. With less fear that we will be overwhelmed by loneliness, we begin to look forward to a quiet evening or the next day. Hope of recovery increases, and the desire to move on is steady and strong. We find longer spaces of peace and contentment. Soon we make it through a whole week and surprise ourselves at not having worried about how we felt. Several months have now elapsed since we said good-bye. Tears are nearly absent.

Holding on to the Past

Occasionally we become reluctant to part with a broken relationship. We struggle to accept the reality that the relationship is ended. We deny any evidence that our partner has declared the relationship ended, and we insist on maintaining contact with a former friend, fiancee, or lover. What we may be experiencing, then, are symptoms of unhealthy grief.

How can we know when we are struggling with unhealthy grief? Getting stuck in a cycle of painful feelings for prolonged periods of time is our first clue. Grief takes time, but it usually is a progressive a process toward healing. The intensity of relationships may affect the length of the grieving process; nonetheless, the process moves towards healing. But destructive grief does not allow us to complete the healing process.

We may become so attached (dependent) in relationships that we resolve not to move on with our lives when they end. This often is the result of one-sided relationships, where one partner's identity and self-worth are wrapped up in the other. Separation is no less than devastating for the dependent partner.

One way of assessing how well we are processing our grief is by sharing our sorrow and our story with an honest friend. Candid and straightforward friends are good allies during painful disengagement—and are only improved upon by a professional counselor who can provide us with a more objective view. Genuine people tell us the truth about any unhealthy behaviors or actions, and help us see ourselves through the eyes of others. Counselors and parish ministers are in the best position to tell us when we are dwelling on issues too long, or when we are focusing on ourselves to the point that our grief work is harmful.

Delayed Grief

Occasionally we do not experience the full impact of sorrow until weeks or months after a relationship has ended. It is not uncommon for people who are juggling great amounts of stress to postpone feeling their suffering by setting it aside emotionally for a period of time. Sometimes we become relieved when our first reaction to a loss is mild—and congratulate ourselves for doing well. Then a seemingly small issue or event triggers an intense flow of tears and painful emotions—and we are bewildered by our reaction.

The human body is a complex organism that often functions with unusual capacities for adaptation. Sorrows and losses, which could overwhelm us, are sometimes temporarily shelved—as a coping device when we are already emotionally overextended. The internal emotional sensors in our human system then store traumatic losses and release their power when our capacity for processing them is restored.

When seemingly unrelated or unimportant issues evoke deep sadness and tears, we need not be disappointed with ourselves. Chances are, we have just given ourselves permission to deal with the full impact of a loss. Such feelings will not overwhelm us; rather, they will provide us relief from the burden of carrying the heavy weight of loss.

When we experience surprising feelings of sadness that seem unrelated to an immediate crisis, the best thing to do is to let those feelings of expression take their course. Talking and crying will help release them. Delayed sorrow is normal, and its appearance is probably a sign that our burdened self is ready to let them out.

Give Sorrow Time

Our tears of sorrow are valuable expressions of care. They manifest our capacity to love and our sadness at the interruption of love. Created to become an integral part of someone else's life, we bond in a vital way to one another, and to God. The experience of losing that "connectedness" is the occasion for significant personal loss. Processing that loss takes time.

We must give sorrow time. Learning to love takes time and letting go of love is a sacred, deliberate journey. We will probably love again; but no love is like any other, and our tears of sorrow affirm the wonder and uniqueness of having cared for someone who became very dear to us—someone we miss.

Chapter 12

———•———

When There Are No Tears

Sometimes the joy, sometimes the pain,
Sometimes the words, sometimes the tears;
Sometimes the grief, sometimes the calm,
Sometimes the dark , sometimes the fears;
Sometimes the hope . . .

M OST OF US KNOW THE UNEASY, INTERNAL SENSATION that alerts us to intense emotions. We also know the strange feeling of wanting to cry, but being unable to do so. Sometimes there are no tears. What does the absence of our tears mean?

Numbness

Any student of human grief will quickly remember that shock and numbness often preside over our initial emotional reactions. Shock and numbness are defenses against traumatic or disheartening news. A merciful God has protected us with a measure of anesthesia that limits and coats our pain. This explains why much of the grief we face is, in fact, delayed grief. The angry tears of abuse victims are sometimes delayed, and so are the tears of loneliness and failure.

When tears are not immediately evident, we may be misunderstood. Some people mistake the lack of tears for absence of grief. But many people steel themselves emotionally during painful ordeals. People who really know and care for us know this and, during such "anesthetic" moments, do not to push us emotionally. We ourselves will know when we can outwardly express our feelings. In the meantime, we need patience and understanding from a faith community that will walk the painful emotional journey with us.

Tears will come soon enough. When they do, they may surprise us by showing up in unexpected places or unpredictable moments. Tears have their own schedule, what might be called the "timing of the soul."

Some of us wait to cry because of our role as the "stabilizer" in the family. During personal crises, some families come apart and turn to the most stable family members for calm, perspective, and stability. When we take on this role in our family, we are often expected to be the last one to cry, or the last one to show any emotions that might suggest that we are out of control.

Stabilizers usually postpone their tears until other family members have expressed their distress and regained their composure. When everyone is back into their routines or have returned home, then, and only then, do stabilizers let down their guard and shed postponed tears. Even then, some of us, as stabilizers, will cry only during secluded moments.

Exhaustion

Sometimes we are too exhausted to cry. When events have worn us down and stress has been a constant burden, we may come to a place where tears are gone. Or when pain is fierce and fatigue is deep, our systems slow and give us time to regain some balance. Breathing decreases and muscles relax. Our weary eyes must rest before they cry again.

The interruption of our tears is a temporary interlude in an intense struggle. We will cry again. But for now, we need to accept the restful moments without tears. Our numbness may alarm us, but we need not fear. Our grieving bodies just need rest.

This interruption should never be confused with the end of our struggles; it is simply our bodies' response to limitations on the length of active trauma they can tolerate. We may need to interpret our situation to friends so they can understand how exhausting such an experience can be.

Fear

Sometimes old fears prevent the flow of tears. If we are afraid of being hurt or rejected or, if we have been punished for crying, we may control our tears to avoid additional harm. The sexually abused daughter of a minister with whom I counseled explained her controlled facial expression to me by telling me that she could be "thrashed" for showing tears.

Some men were told as boys that they should never cry. Afraid of being labeled "sissies," some of us have choked out our tears. We have learned to turn away, to lower our heads, to tighten our jaws and grit our teeth—all to avoid crying when we are afraid, in pain, or lonely. And after rehearsing every conceivable way to avoid crying, we learned how to disguise crying by coughing, clearing our throats, walking away, or raising our voices. Sometimes our disguises work; other times they do not.

For all our effort, we still shed tears and feel ashamed and ridiculous. We may believe that crying is a weakness. We fear that people will think we have no control or that we will be labeled "soft-hearted."

Some of us fear there is so much anger, pain, or frustration inside us that should be start crying, we might not stop. Such a myth develops because we have ignored or postponed vital feelings. But rather than overwhelm us, expressed feelings will free us from using so much energy to contain or control our emotions. Letting our pent-up turmoil go—and releasing held-back tears—may start a torrent of spilled emotions, but they will soon subside.

Anger

We have also controlled our tears out of anger. Prisoners in concentration camps during World War II described the atrocities and torture they witnessed—and the pleasure their tears seemed to bring their captors. Several of them resolved to harness their tears as long as they could to deprive their captors of any additional satisfaction.

Sometimes we experience degrading and appalling behaviors and our wounded bodies decide that they will not surrender the last act over which we may have control: our emotions. Some people have commanded every ounce of control within their bodies to avoid crying. Abused women and children, for example, often learn to swallow tears.

As wounded spirits we have also camouflaged our tears during long bouts of mistreatment and injustice. We have seen the tearless faces of minorities, robbed for years of decency and respect. Hopefully we recognize the hollow stare of those who have been victimized to the point of detachment. Angry and rejected over and over, these children of neglect have grown up in bitterness and suspicion. Any of us who have experienced abuse or exploitation know that victims of abuse reach a point in their mistreatment when tears stop and anger becomes a permanent companion.

The absence of our tears is an angry response to injustice. No one should confuse our lack of tears for lack of feeling. Tears simply cannot fully express our internal anguish. Buried deep inside us are memories of episodic mistreatment and hostility. Layered over these memories are the learned feelings of alienation and apathy. Beneath the apathy is a desire to hide the seething agony, which seemingly matters to no one. So there are no tears; the tears ended long ago. When they ceased to express the depth of our anguish, we learned to stifle our tears.

Detachment

A tearless life can reflect a very troubled journey. For example, abused, betrayed, and battered infants often develop an "emotional apathy" in order to survive. We become detached emotionally from life; an uneasy calm settles over us. Our tears brought us no compassion; our well-being was of interest to no one; our wounds were no one's obligation. We learned to ignore our feelings—and the feelings of others.

When we grow up believing that our feelings never mattered, we emerge as adults believing also that no one else's feelings matter either. Because no one bothered with our tears, we now have no tears left to cry. Devoid of feelings we can recognize in ourselves, we have little understanding of the feelings of others.

Some of us who can no longer cry have developed a permanent marginal posture. To protect us from emotional connection, we distance ourselves from all who might hurt us, ignore us, or neglect us. It's lonely, but it protects us from emotional harm. We have ceased to cry not because we have ceased to care; but because we cared—and hurt—too much.

There are many good reasons for our tears to fail us. Each may alter the natural appearance of our tears. If, for whatever reason, our tears do not return over time, we may need to seek professional help. Tearless days are to be expected in the struggles we have described. The delay or absence of tears can allow us healing and perspective. But if our tears stop altogether, we have lost a valuable emotional language of our souls.

> Sometimes I wish for a tear in my eye—
> Sometimes I wish I'd never cry;
> Sometimes I wish my tears could speak
> and name the things my heart still seeks.

Conclusion: Making Tears Our Friends

Throughout this book, the message has been that our tears are valuable. They are a gesture of trust. With our tears we allow others to see deeper into the dimensions of our lives. Through tears we express our hopes, fears, and passions. They are like a bridge that unites the inner and outer selves.

Our tears are instruments of cleansing and release. They draw toxin and tension from our bodies. They warn us of our needs, alert us to our vulnerability, and heal our emotional wounds. Tears allow us to see issues and concerns more clearly.

Tears express issues. With our tears we express the harmful anger that otherwise would remain locked in our bodies. With tears, we confess our faults and limitations, which gives us opportunity to atone and start over. Tears help us identify our failures, declare fatigue, manage frustration, and confront fear.

With tears we express our gratitude for unexpected grace, and give voice to our loneliness and isolation in the challenge of daily living. Tears give us permission to meet legitimate human needs without manipulation: We learn to ask for affection, attention, care, respect, and value. Our tears can also express compassion and support without control or deceit. They help state our pain and suffering. Tears allow us the time to acknowledge hurt and to heal.

Tears help interpret our sorrows during times of great loss. Weeping is a powerful language that lends understanding, strength, and color to our passions. May the language of tears provide windows through which we share our treasured selves with those we love, and may our knowledge of tears bring us closer to one another in our journey of self-understanding and faith.